Centerville
Washington-Cent
Centerville, Ohio

W9-ARJ-128

Centennial Library
Washington-Centerville Public Library
Centerville, Ohio

THANKSGIVING

THANKSGIVING

How to Cook It Well

SAM SIFTON

Illustrations by Sarah C. Rutherford

RANDOM HOUSE 🏛 NEW YORK

Copyright © 2012 by Sam Sifton

Illustrations copyright © 2012 by Sarah C. Rutherford

All rights reserved.

Published in the United States by Random House,
an imprint of The Random House Publishing Group,
a division of Random House, Inc., New York.

RANDOM HOUSE and colophon are registered trademarks of
Random House, Inc.

Library of Congress Cataloging-in-Publication Data
Sifton, Sam.
Thanksgiving : how to cook it well / Sam Sifton.
p. cm.
Includes index.
Summary: "From one of America's finest food writers, the former restaurant critic for
The New York Times, comes a definitive, timeless guide to Thanksgiving dinner—
preparing it, surviving it, and pulling it off in style. From the planning of the meal to
the washing of the last plate, Thanksgiving poses more—and more vexing—problems
for the home cook than any other holiday. In this smartly written, beautifully
illustrated, recipe-filled book, Sam Sifton, the *Times's* resident Thanksgiving
expert, delivers a message of great comfort and solace: There is no need for fear. You can cook
a great meal on Thanksgiving. You can have a great time. With simple, foolproof
recipes for classic Thanksgiving staples, as well as new takes on old standbys, this
book will show you that the fourth Thursday of November does not have to be a day
of kitchen stress and family drama, of dry stuffing and sad, cratered pies. You can
make a better turkey than anyone has ever served you in your life, and you can serve
it with gravy that is not lumpy or bland but a salty balm, rich in flavor, that transforms
all it touches. Here are recipes for exciting side dishes and robust pies and festive
cocktails, instructions for setting the table and setting the mood, as well as cooking
techniques and menu ideas that will serve you all year long, whenever you are
throwing a big party. Written for novice and experienced cooks alike, *Thanksgiving:
How to Cook It Well* is your guide to making Thanksgiving the best holiday of the
year. It is not fantasy. If you prepare, it will happen. And this book will show you
how"—Provided by publisher.
ISBN 978-1-4000-6991-0 (hardback)—ISBN 978-0-679-60514-0 (ebook)
1. Thanksgiving cooking. 2. Cooking, American. I. Title.
TX739.2.T45S54 2012
641.5′68—dc23
2012013919

Printed in the United States of America on acid-free paper

www.atrandom.com

2 4 6 8 9 7 5 3

Book design by Liz Cosgrove

For my mom, who taught me to give thanks

CONTENTS

THANKSGIVING

INTRODUCTION

THANKSGIVING IS NOT EASY. The holiday is for many of us a day of travel, of traffic and stress. It is a day of hot ovens, increasingly drunk uncles and crowded dinner tables, of people arriving late or needing to leave early, of burned yams and spouses who forgot to buy the one thing—the one thing!—you asked them not to forget to buy. Thanksgiving can be a hard day to manage. It takes strength.

The cooking can be difficult. (That turkey is so big, and your oven so small.) The interpersonal dynamics are often harder. [Cue tears.] Either you are traveling somewhere to be fed, or opening your home to people in order to feed them. This is not easy, ever. You may be putting feuds on hold or building bridges between clans. You may be sharing family traditions or creating them or fighting against them or all three at once.

I can help. I have spent the last 25 years cooking Thanksgivings in homes real and improvised. I have cooked with and for the family I was born into, for the ones I built with friends, for the families my parents married into after they ceased to be married to each other, and for the one I created with my wife and children. I have run Thanksgivings for two people and for dozens. I have seen a lot of birds.

For a couple of years I spent Thanksgiving Day at *The New York Times*, where I once was restaurant critic and now work as national editor, answering panicked questions from readers. I was a one-man Thanksgiving help line. The questions came fast and furious, in email messages sent from all over the country and from all over the world. I answered questions on the newspaper's website about burning turkeys and still-frozen ones, bland gravies and last-minute cranberry sauces, too-thick corn puddings, underdone squash, what to do with someone's vegan aunt or carnivorous boss.

Once, someone asked me how to cook bush meat. (Carefully.) Another time, someone wanted to know what to tell the cook running the tandoor oven near his home in Mumbai, since the guy had never before seen a turkey. (Tell him it's a big chicken?) I consulted on failed pumpkin pies and epic turducken blunders. I worked the turkey-oven-temperature-time equation as if studying for a doctoral exam.

I saw the depths to which some cooks can fall during Thanksgiving, and I bore witness to the heights to which some cooks have risen.

And all along I asked questions of experts and tested their advice at home. I have brined turkeys and not brined them, smoked turkeys, fried turkeys, roasted them upside down, right side up, covered in butter-soaked cheesecloth, at high temperatures and at low. I have whipped potatoes and baked potatoes and applied marshmallows to yams, parboiled green beans and wok-fried Brussels sprouts. I have cut turkeys up to speed the cooking process. I've made turkey mole. I have experimented in your name.

This book compiles all that I have learned. It is a primer. It should provide you with solace as you face the terrors of your first Thanksgiving or the boredom of your 26th. And it will, I hope, answer any and all questions you have about the day and its preparation, its beginnings, its middle, its end. Thanksgiving, after all, always brings questions, doubts, and emergencies. This book exists to answer and assuage them and, if necessary, to apply electric paddles to chests. It is a Thanksgiving ambulance in book form.

You can go your whole life and then wake up one morning and look in the refrigerator at this animal carcass the size of a toddler and think: *I have to cook that today.*

There is no need to worry. Thanksgiving does not have to be a drag. It does not have to involve dry turkey or scorched potatoes, chalky stuffing or a cousin in from Erie weeping in the hall. There is no need to argue. There is no need for fear. You can cook a great meal on Thanksgiving. You can have a great time.

This is my testimony: You can make a better turkey than anyone has ever served you in your life. You can serve it with dressing that will make your guests swoon.

You can make Brussels sprouts into something marvelous. They need not be mush, nor taste of soap. Your gravy can be a salty balm, rich in flavor, transforming all that it touches. You can have cranberry sauce that does not come out of a can; sweet potatoes free of marshmallows; butternut squash with maple and bacon, chipotle, and butter; mashed potatoes thick with cream. You can have crisp green beans, a beautiful pecan pie.

You can make all this and your family can gather in happiness around you to consume it. (And they can watch television while they wait. Yes, they can. Football is part of this holiday, too.) There can be a fire if you have the place for it, or just roaring conversation to warm the heart, as kids do jigsaw puzzles on the floor, if you don't.

This is not fantasy. If you prepare, it will happen.

And then there will be a meal, and with it joy at the cold tart taste of cranberry licking at warm, silky turkey meat, as candles flicker in a draft from the door. There should be napkins, too, real ones, and a walk after you eat, and then dogs asleep on the rug or a cat asleep on your lap. There ought to be laughter throughout. For whoever comes into your home, whoever you invite, whoever invites himself, whoever needs to be invited, whoever's there: Thanksgiving ought to be the best holiday of the year.

You need only cook the meal correctly, and clean up before you go to bed.

This book is going to tell you how to make that happen. This book is going to make it possible for you to cook Thanksgiving and not lose your mind. It is going to help you build family traditions, or alter old ones. It will, at the same time, show you how to have fun in the kitchen, how to improvise and innovate, and when you are done, how to serve your food in such a way that it makes the holiday entirely your own.

You are going to page through this book—read and digest, argue and discuss, make plans and write lists—and then you are going to cook and serve a meal that will bring praise down upon you like showers of rose petals.

The history of Thanksgiving is one filled with myth and heartache. Our not-yet-nation's first holiday feast, at Plymouth Plantation in 1621, was a celebration of the British separatists' first successful harvest there and a gesture of thanks to the Wampanoag man who helped them achieve it against heavy odds. (Raise a glass to Squanto, kids!) It wasn't much: venison and wild turkey, some sea ducks, some cod. There was wheat, barley, corn, squash, some bowls of beans. There were no potatoes. No marshmallows. No tender cocktail onions to cream.

Those early Americans gave the meal a pass the next year, and for years that followed, as you might have too, after a bowl of barley and a rare breast of sea duck. For more than 200 years, in fact, the holiday was celebrated only spasmodically by individual colonies and states. These were harvest celebrations, mostly, more impromptu party than national tradition. They offered a chance for settlers to rest and reflect, to give thanks to God and luck.

Only at a nadir of the nation's history, with states torn by the rancor and violence of civil war, did Abraham Lincoln, in October 1863, use the office of his presidency to declare a national day of Thanksgiving. This was a day, he said, meant to return to our people notions of "peace, harmony, tranquility and Union." Yet still, Thanksgiving did not become a national holiday until 1941, when Congress sanctioned it so: the fourth Thursday of every November. Two years later, as war raged in Europe, Norman Rockwell's painting "Freedom From Want" was published on the cover of the *Saturday Evening Post*, helping cement the image of Thanksgiving as a formal family meal.

It is against that background—kindly Granny serving a massive bird as kids and grandkids smile in their Sunday best—that the modern holiday looms. Thanks to Rockwell and Roosevelt, and thanks, too, to Lincoln and Squanto, this is the case wherever Americans live. We are a young nation still, and love our secular pageantry. Despite regional differences (and glorious ones at that), Thanksgiving is essentially the same whether you observe it in Manhattan or in Montana, Key West, or Terre Haute. It is a celebration of American excess and of American friendship, in all its many guises.

Thanksgiving says: In trailer homes and mansions alike, we are a nation of good fortune and happiness. Everybody digs in.

But be forewarned. *Thanksgiving* is not a book for everyone. It is not for those in search of the new Thanksgiving craze, the latest recipe for turkey in a bag, the next big trend in holiday entertaining. There will be no recipes here for ham or lamb, roast beef or swordfish. Thanksgiving is a holiday that anchors itself in tradition. Which means: You will make a turkey. Turkey is why you are here.

Thanksgiving is likewise not a book for those interested in cutting corners. Shortcuts are anathema to Thanksgiving, which is a holiday that celebrates not just our bounty but also our slow, careful preparation of it. There is no room in Thanksgiving for the false wisdom of compromise—for ways to celebrate the holiday without cooking, or by cranking open cans of gravy to pour over a store-roasted turkey reheated in the microwave. Thanksgiving is no place for irony. We are simply going to cook.

Put plainly, we are going to cook Thanksgiving *correctly.*

And what exactly does that mean? It means there is going to

be a turkey, and side dishes and dressing to go with it, and plenty of gravy as well. There is going to be a proper dinner table even if it turns out to be a slab of plywood over some milk crates, covered by a sheet. There are going to be proper place settings for each person and glasses for water and wine. There are going to be candles. There will be dessert.

It means there will not be salad at meal's end, or appetizers at its beginning. Please understand that from the very beginning. There can be a soup course at Thanksgiving if you wish, some delicate oyster bisque or creamy squash to guard against the chill of advancing winter. But you should not be filling a Thanksgiving guest's stomach with onion tarts or nuts or corn chips or wee little *amuses bouches* in advance of a trencherman's feast of turkey and four sides, the whole thing covered with gravy. Appetizers may promote the appetite of those who order and consume them in restaurants. At Thanksgiving, though, appetizers take up valuable stomach space. They are insulting to your own hard work.

And salad? No. See above. A salad is a perfect accompaniment to many meals, a hit of astringency that can improve some dinners hugely. Not this one. You can have your salad tomorrow.

Finally, this: We should all celebrate Thanksgiving and we should all strive to make it great. The holiday is not always perfect. It does not always work out. But it comes every year with promise and possibility, and this book is going to help you get closer to happiness and cheer than you have ever gotten in the past. Everything will be all right.

This most of all is the message of *Thanksgiving*: Everything really will be all right.

CHAPTER ONE

GETTING STARTED

Y OU DO NOT NEED a restaurant-quality kitchen to cook Thanksgiving properly. You probably have most of the equipment you need already. But there are a few tools and supplies that will make the journey easier. Here are the absolute essentials.

1. THE KITCHEN

Pots and Pans

HEAVY-BOTTOMED POTS AND PANS of various sizes are crucial for a successful Thanksgiving. The very first thing you are going to do on Thanksgiving morning is pull the turkey neck from the carcass of the bird you are going to cook and use it to start a small stock that will bubble all day in a corner of the stove, ready for use as a dressing moisturizer, or meat heater, or gravy enhancer. And you are going to need a pot for that. (See page 19.)

You are going to need another pot to melt butter, or to keep your basting sauce warm. You will make cranberry sauce in a pot. You may blanch green beans in one. Potatoes for mashing will cook in a pot, and probably something else as well. And you will need pans to brown sausage for dressing, or to glaze carrots, or to fry Brussels sprouts or make gravy. The list can get long.

The pots and pans need not be expensive, and they certainly may be borrowed from friends or brought by relatives. But the pots all should have lids, and ideally heavy bottoms that heat evenly, without hot spots that can cause scorching. (Those enameled cast-iron numbers that people give for wedding presents are far and away the best.) As for pans, I prefer heavy stainless or cast-iron. But you should have tasted the parsnips I made one year in a battered nonstick pan of supermarket heritage that someone found under a sink, its handle covered in rust. That dish was perfect. So long as you are careful with it, even a cheap pan can perform like an expensive one.

Of course, you are going to need something in which to cook the turkey, and in which to roast vegetables and cook the dressing. I have huge French-style roasting pans—big, heavy pans with high sides and racks that I use to cook roasts and vegetables. (You get married, you can have these things as well.) To make gravy, I sometimes pull the meat from the pan and let it rest on a platter, then put the pan itself on my stovetop and use it as I would a sauté pan.

Huge French-style roasting pans are great. But they are not necessary. What *is* necessary: a pan that is larger than the bird you are going to cook, with sides high enough to contain the drippings that bird is going to give off during the process of cooking it, and enough strength to hold the bird without collapsing when you take it out of the oven.

You can get one of these pans at the supermarket for about what it costs to buy a quart of milk: a throwaway aluminum roasting pan. If you are cooking a turkey larger than 15 pounds, buy two pans and place one inside the other. These pans are not ideal, in part because they are not rigid, and in part because they do not come with those big V-shaped racks that hold the turkey above the cooking surface, which allows for uniform browning. But they are not awful. They work. Simply line the area that will be underneath the turkey with a small bed of thick-sliced onions to keep the skin from sticking as you roast.

Other things you will need roasting pans for during Thanksgiving: dressing; butternut squash; sweet potatoes; Brussels sprouts; anything you wish to brown in the high heat of the oven. A roasting pan that is too small to hold the turkey can come in handy here, as can smaller throwaway versions from the market, which can be reused after dinner for leftovers and eventual reheating.

Give thanks for aluminum, then, but also plan. Sketch out a menu on a piece of paper and figure for each dish what kind of pot or pan you are going to need to make it, and when in the course of the day. This will give you some sense of whether you are going to need to call cousin Janie and borrow her Dutch oven for the sprouts.

Hand Tools

TAKE A BRIEF RUN through your kitchen cabinets. You should have: wooden spoons for stirring and a narrow kitchen fork or pair of tongs for poking and turning things. You will benefit from having a ladle or big spoon for dealing with drippings, and a colander in which to drain potatoes and green beans. (You don't need a baster, though they're nice.) A nest of mixing bowls is also a good thing to have, for mixing ingredients for the dressing, or to hold apples sliced for the pie, or for draining off stock, or both.

And of course you will need something with which to mash potatoes, for a Thanksgiving without mashed potatoes is hardly a Thanksgiving at all. I use a stand mixer, which brings a nice whipped quality to the dish, but it is not a tool everyone has, nor one that everyone needs. I have mashed potatoes with a fork. It takes a long time. Better to invest in a sturdy potato masher. It will pay dividends for years.

Knives

THERE IS A LOT of peeling and chopping and cutting to Thanksgiving, even before the bird comes to the table, so you will need knives. At the end of the day, you will need a carving knife for the turkey—something long and thin and sharp. You will need a peeler for the carrots and the squash and the potatoes. You may also desire a paring knife, for messing with apples or chestnuts.

But the most important knife to have at Thanksgiving is a chef's knife, which means a knife of between 8 and 10 inches in length, with a wide blade.

There are three main shapes for these. French chef's knives have relatively straight blades, with only a small curve to their sharp edge. They resemble long triangles. German-style chef's knives have more curvature. They resemble closed lobster claws. Japanese santoku knives, in contrast, have what's called a sheep's-foot shape, for the drop at the knife's tip from the dull side to the cutting edge.

Which of these knives is best for Thanksgiving has little to do with the cost of the knife. It has everything to do with how the knives feel in your hand, and how comfortable you are using them in a variety of tasks. Knife selection is a business of trial and error. I have some wickedly expensive German and Japanese knives. They are beautiful tools, hold their edges well, have amazing balance in my hand. But I do not use them nearly as much as I do the cheap, plastic-handled 8-inch chef's knife I bought in a commercial kitchen supply store 20 years ago for $8 and that now costs $19 online. It has never let me down.

Cutting Boards

A HEAVY-DUTY PLASTIC CUTTING board the size of your local newspaper is a marvelous thing for a daylong cooking project like Thanksgiving because it is easily cleaned and nonabsorbent. But those old wooden butcher blocks and grandma's carving boards will work, too. Just clean them as you go, between every task. This is the most important thing to do as you cook, for reasons of both mental and physical health. Keep your work area clean, always.

2. THE PANTRY

THERE ARE REASONS WHY restaurant food tastes better than the food we cook at home. Two of them are salt and pepper. A third is fat. Restaurant cooks use all three with a heavier hand than most home cooks, with the result that their food often has bigger, more intense flavor than anything cooked at home. Those big flavors, and an accompanying buttery richness, can help mark the occasion of dining out as a special one, different from other days and meals.

Thanksgiving is different from other days and meals. You ought to prepare for it, right from the start.

Salt and Pepper

ALL THE RECIPES IN this book call for and were tested with coarse salt, often known as kosher salt: thick-grained, irregularly sized, and easily pinched, with real texture. (Compare with sea salt, if you like, but sea salt is generally more expensive.) Of course you can use table salt—the thin, iodized stuff of fast-food salt packets—but know that because of its tiny crystals there is much more salt in a single teaspoon of the iodized variety than in a single teaspoon of its coarse cousin. Iodized salt tastes sharper and saltier on the tongue, and it lacks crunch as well. Some bakers revere it for how easily it dissolves. But for the purposes of Thanksgiving, we shall remain steadfast and coarse.

The flavor of black pepper is best when it is freshly ground. All kitchens should have a pepper grinder, and if that is the case you might as well make it a good one. That is a good thing to tell yourself, anyway, when you come home with a nickel-plated cast-aluminum pepper mill from Perfex that costs about what dinner for two would run in the sort of restaurant where jackets are required. Still, you can get a perfectly good pepper grinder at a housewares store for less than the cost of an airport meal. Do so.

Butter

LET US SPEAK PLAINLY: you are going to need a lot of butter. Thanksgiving is not a day for diets, or for worrying about your cholesterol. It is a day on which we celebrate the delicious. And there is precious little on a Thanksgiving menu that is not made more delicious by butter.

And so your refrigerator should be filled with butter, as fresh as you can get, as nice as you can afford. We will use butter on and in the turkey, and to baste the bird throughout the day. We will use it in mashed potatoes, mashed sweet potatoes, on other vegetables, in desserts. Butter is to the Thanksgiving larder as olive oil is to the everyday Italian one: an indispensable fat, and an incredible conductor of flavor. It acts as through-line for the day.

It ought to be unsalted butter. There is something magical about a piece of toast spread with salted butter. But for cooking Thanksgiving, you want the unsalted variety, so that it is you, and not the butter maker, who is in control of the saltiness of your cooking. Figure at least two pounds for the day. There may well be lots left over, to be sure, depending on what you cook. But two pounds sends a message.

Herbs, Spices, and Flavoring Agents

FOR THE RECIPES IN this book, rosemary, sage, and thyme predominate, along with the chopped parsley you can use to finish almost every platter you send out to the table. (It looks pretty and offers a clean, bright flavor against the butter.) Cut these from your window box or garden if you have such a thing, or buy sprigs at the market on the day before Thanksgiving and keep them cool in the refrigerator, their stems immersed in a glass of water.

You will want as well to have on hand fresh spices that evoke the season, and the warmth and comfort we seek during it: cinnamon and cloves, nutmeg, and some red pepper flakes just because.

You will need onions, as well: a goodly couple of pounds at least. I like big Spanish ones for their intense and consistent flavor. Also, shallots: a close relative of the onion, smaller, somewhat sweeter and richer in taste, good for the base of a gravy or to top the green beans. You will not need garlic. There is little place in Thanksgiving for garlic. It has a pungent, spicy flavor that mellows as it cooks, and it is fantastically delicious 364 days a year. But you will not need it on Thanksgiving, where it debases mashed potatoes and brings turkey meat low.

Flour and Sugar

THANKSGIVING REQUIRES PLENTY OF all-purpose flour and plain white sugar, and you should lay in stocks accordingly, along with a tin of baking powder. But brown sugar, smoky and more richly flavored than white, is often used in the Thanksgiving kitchen as well, where it enhances squashes and pies alike. (I also keep on hand molasses and maple syrup, for similar reasons.)

Some families (mine, for instance) require cornmeal, which we use to make the cornbread at the center of our dressing. Others need biscuit flour or Bisquick, though Bisquick is pushing things in a direction that you do not want to go. It is a slippery slope from there to canned cranberry sauce and from there to the dreaded bag of marshmallows.

All Thanksgiving cooks should purchase instant flour, usually found in the supermarket in a sleeve marked "Wondra." Instant flour is low in protein, and it dissolves quickly and smoothly in liquids, regardless of temperature. It makes terrible pie crusts and bread, but as a thickening agent for gravies, it really cannot be beat.

Stock

HAVING A LOT OF turkey stock on hand is crucial to the preparation of a good Thanksgiving meal. It ought to be the first thing you prepare, in fact, on Thursday morning, if not before. Supplemented with homemade or store-bought low-sodium chicken stock, this elixir will be a central ingredient in your gravy. You can use it to revitalize dry oven-cooked dressings and sliced white-meat turkey as well. Turkey stock is a Thanksgiving secret weapon.

———— QUICK TURKEY STOCK ————

Turkey neck
1 Spanish onion, peeled and cut in half
1 large carrot, peeled and cut into large pieces
1 stalk celery, cleaned and cut into large pieces

1. Put neck, onion, carrot, and celery in a medium-sized pot and cover with cold water.

2. Place the pot over high heat and bring to a boil. Reduce heat and simmer all day.

THE FINAL TURKEY STOCK

YOU MAY BELIEVE YOU are done with your turkey when the last shred of meat comes off its carcass, some time after the holiday has passed. But you are just starting your journey. A turkey stripped of meat signals time to make a final turkey stock of the holiday, which works beautifully for gumbo, soup, beans—for any recipe where you might otherwise require a chicken stock.

The recipe is simplicity itself. Take what remains of your bird and break it up so that it can fit into a large stockpot. Add to the pot three stalks of roughly chopped celery and a large Spanish onion cut into quarters, then cover with water. Put the pot on your stove over high heat until it comes to a boil, then reduce heat to a bare simmer and cook, barely stirring, for at least four hours, or overnight. In time the bones will release their marrow and roasted flavor, imparting to the stock a dark and incomparable heartiness.

SERIOUS TURKEY STOCK

2 turkey drumsticks
2 turkey wings
2 large Spanish onions, peeled and cut in half
2 large carrots, peeled and cut into large pieces
2 stalks celery, cut into large pieces
2 bay leaves
3 sprigs fresh thyme
1 tablespoon cracked black peppercorns

1. Preheat oven to 400 degrees. Place turkey parts in a large pan and cook in the oven until they are golden, with the skin beginning to separate from the end of the drumsticks, approximately 30 minutes.

2. Transfer turkey parts and all accumulated fat and juices to a large stockpot. Cover turkey with water and place the pot on the stovetop. Turn heat to high and bring water to a boil, then reduce heat, cover, and simmer for as long as you can manage, even overnight.

3. Add the vegetables, bay leaves, thyme, and pepper and continue to cook for another hour, then strain stock into a clean container. Cover and place in refrigerator. When cool, pull off the layer of fat on top and discard. Reheat on Thanksgiving morning, and use all day.

CHAPTER TWO

THE TURKEY

THE FIRST THANKSGIVING I took a significant part in cooking was when I was 20, a college kid working at a restaurant and living in a big, rambling apartment close to the good part of town. A group of us lived there, assembled under the lease of our oldest member, a graduate student. The apartment was a kind of Dickensian club devoted to a perennially shifting list of priorities that generally included music, books, girls, sports, cigarettes, beer, and food.

We slept on couches and watched Headline News. On Thanksgiving, we cooked turkey.

We woke up early and slid a massive supermarket bird into the balky oven. We made coffee and lists, then proceeded to shop and cook and drink wine, and watch football and cut jokes at one another as the roasting turkey filled the whole house with an ambrosial scent, enough to overpower the stench of men who were really no more than boys. Then we set out a table of sawhorses and plywood, and covered it in cloth and candles and mismatched china and silverware, and some girls came over and there was turkey and gravy and stuffing and sides.

The meat was moist beneath its crisp and burnished skin, the potatoes creamy, the cranberries tart, the gravy not so lean. There was wine and more wine on top of that. Candles winked in a draft and music played in the other room, someone's mixtape: perfection on a loop.

I have forgotten the conversations. But never the meal. I have been cooking that Thanksgiving turkey ever since.

The recipe calls for a glaze: a kind of rosemary-infused teriyaki butter. My friend John Montano used it during that first Thanksgiving all that time ago, and it was good enough that I have used it ever since. It is not necessary, strictly speaking. You could use plain butter or a combination of butter and herbs instead.

But the aroma that wafted through the house for the duration of that first college Thanksgiving was and remains incredible to me. The piney rosemary combines beautifully with the butter and turkey fat and the zing of soy sauce and the sweet caramel scent of the sugars in the mirin browning on the skin. It is familiar and exotic at once. And it results in flavor of astonishing depth: the turkey meat sweet and pure beneath its lacquered exterior, the skin slightly salty and herbaceous.

Of course, there are literally hundreds of ways to cook a Thanksgiving turkey. You could boil a turkey if you wanted to. You could roast it upside down for a time and hope that this keeps the breast meat juicy. You could wrap the bird in moistened cheesecloth and cook it in a convection oven. You could cut it into pieces and cook it in parts. You could smoke it. Fry it. Shred its legs into sauce. You could even put a turkey on a

stick set under a clean tin garbage can in the backyard and cover
the top with coals, as the Boy Scouts do sometimes, though this
is hard to picture and harder still to do. You could stuff it and
roast it or you could roast it and not stuff it, and make the dressing on the side. If the result tastes good, it is a correct way to
cook the Thanksgiving bird.

In the coming pages, we will look at a few of the best meth-
ods for doing that.

But the best recipe to start with is the easiest and most
straightforward of all: You simply roast the bird in a hot oven
for 30 minutes, then lower the heat and allow it to crank along
slowly, 15 minutes per pound, until it is done. Baste the meat
every 30 minutes. And use a thermometer to make sure that you
do not overcook the meat.

That's it. Give thanks!

—— A SIMPLE ROAST TURKEY ——

*1 12- to 18-pound turkey, thawed, with giblets and
    neck removed*
3 tablespoons kosher salt
1½ tablespoons freshly ground black pepper
6 tablespoons unsalted butter, softened
1 medium onion, peeled and quartered
2 stalks celery, cleaned and roughly chopped
3 tablespoons soy sauce
1 tablespoon mirin
3 sprigs fresh rosemary
1 cup turkey stock (pages 19 and 21) or water

1. Heat oven to 425 degrees. Rinse turkey and dry carefully with paper towels. Rub the bird inside and out with salt and pepper and place in roasting pan fitted with a rack. Rub 3 table-spoons butter over the top of the turkey. Place vegetables into cavity. Tuck the tips of the wings under the bird.

2. Meanwhile, melt the remaining 3 tablespoons butter in a small pan with soy sauce and mirin (you can substitute a commercial teriyaki sauce for these liquids), add rosemary, and stir. Keep warm on stove, but do not allow to boil.

3. Pour stock or water into the pan, beneath the bird. Put turkey in oven and roast, uncovered, for 30 minutes, then reduce temperature to 325 degrees and baste turkey with pan juices. After 30 additional minutes, baste again, supplementing the pan juices with a little bit of the butter mixture from the top of the stove. Repeat every 30 minutes.

4. At 325 degrees, the turkey will cook at approximately 15 minutes per pound. (If the turkey starts to get too dark, tent it loosely with aluminum foil.) After a few hours, insert a meat thermometer straight down into fleshiest part of thigh, where it meets the drumstick, and check the temperature. Do not let the thermometer touch the bone. Thigh meat should reach no more than 165 degrees, with juices running clear when you remove the thermometer.

5. When bird has reached desired temperature, remove from oven and let rest for at least 30 minutes, covered in foil. Remove foil and carve.

AN EVEN MORE SIMPLE ROAST TURKEY

For those who balk at the notion of a Thanksgiving turkey scented with teriyaki sauce, here is a version that omits it in favor of the more traditionally American flavors of apple and thyme.

> *1 12- to 18-pound turkey, thawed, with giblets and*
> *neck removed*
> *3 tablespoons kosher salt*
> *1½ tablespoons freshly ground black pepper*
> *6 tablespoons unsalted butter, softened*
> *1 medium onion, peeled and quartered*
> *2 stalks celery, cleaned and roughly chopped*
> *1 apple, preferably firm and sweet, halved*
> *8 sprigs fresh thyme*
> *1 cup turkey stock (page 19), or water mixed with*
> *apple juice*

1. Heat oven to 425 degrees. Rinse turkey and dry carefully with paper towels. Rub the bird inside and out with salt and pepper and place in roasting pan fitted with a rack. Rub 3 tablespoons butter over the top of the turkey, and the remaining 3 tablespoons butter within it. Place vegetables, apple, and thyme into cavity. Tuck the tips of the wings under the bird.

2. Pour stock or water into the pan, beneath the bird. Put turkey in oven and roast, uncovered, for 30 minutes, then re-

duce temperature to 325 degrees and baste turkey with pan juices. After 30 additional minutes, baste again. Repeat every 30 minutes.

3. At 325 degrees, the turkey will cook at approximately 15 minutes per pound. (If the turkey starts to get too dark, tent it loosely with aluminum foil.) After a few hours, insert a meat thermometer straight down into fleshiest part of thigh, where it meets the drumstick, and check the temperature. Do not let the thermometer touch the bone. Thigh meat should reach no more than 165 degrees, with juices running clear when you remove the thermometer.

4. When bird has reached desired temperature, remove from oven and let rest for at least 30 minutes, covered in foil. Remove foil and carve.

——— HERB-ROASTED TURKEY ———

The combination of herbs and citrus provides a delicious, house-filling aroma. Garnish with some remaining sprigs of sage and thyme, but be careful with the rosemary, as a little goes a long way.

> *1 12- to 18-pound turkey, thawed, with giblets and*
> *   neck removed*
> *3 tablespoons kosher salt*
> *1½ tablespoons freshly ground black pepper*
> *6 tablespoons unsalted butter, softened*
> *1 tablespoon fresh sage leaves, minced*
> *1 tablespoon fresh rosemary needles, minced*

1 tablespoon fresh thyme leaves, minced
Zest of 1 lemon
1 medium onion, peeled and quartered
1 orange, quartered
1 lemon, quartered

1. Heat oven to 425 degrees. Rinse turkey and dry carefully with paper towels. Rub the bird inside and out with salt and pepper and place in roasting pan fitted with a rack. Combine butter, herbs, and lemon zest in a small bowl and use a fork to combine. Rub butter over the top of the turkey and within its cavity.

2. Place onion and fruit into the bird's cavity. Tuck the tips of the wings under the bird.

3. Put turkey in oven and roast, uncovered, for 30 minutes, then reduce temperature to 325 degrees and baste turkey with pan juices. After 30 additional minutes, baste again. Repeat every 30 minutes.

4. At 325 degrees, the turkey will cook at approximately 15 minutes per pound. (If the turkey starts to get too dark, tent it loosely with aluminum foil.) After a few hours, insert a meat thermometer straight down into fleshiest part of thigh, where it meets the drumstick, and check the temperature. Do not let the thermometer touch the bone. Thigh meat should reach no more than 165 degrees, with juices running clear when you remove the thermometer.

5. When bird has reached desired temperature, remove from oven and let rest for at least 30 minutes, covered in foil. Remove foil and carve.

A BRINE FOR TURKEY

SUBMERGING A TURKEY IN a solution of salt and sugar and herbs, and allowing osmosis to do its work, is a process called brining: it is meant to result in a moister turkey and it nearly always succeeds. The fashion for brining turkeys before cooking them is a trend that comes and goes, like skinny ties or Blucher moccasins. When I was in college, brining was not in fashion. Then it was. Then it wasn't. Now it sits in culinary limbo, used by some, not by others: debates rage.

Try it and see what you think. A brine can be helpful when the turkey you are cooking is lean and narrow, as heritage birds often are, in order to compensate for the meat's lack of fat. Brining a turkey is also smart when you are cooking turkey on a grill, since basting is not generally part of that process. Use a brine if you suspect that your past turkeys have been too dry, or you have been told, unkindly, that this is the case.

The following brine will infuse a turkey with substantial juiciness in two or three days' time. It is a simple solution of salt and sugar, with a few spices you might add or subtract according to your tastes. As for the salt and sugar, keep the ratio at no more than a half cup of each for every gallon of water you're using. Too much of either makes the meat taste like something purchased from a gas-station deli.

So: salt, sugar, and herbs go into boiling water to dissolve the first two. Allow this solution to cool, then submerge your bird in the result and keep the whole thing chilled until you are ready to cook. If you don't have a refrigerator large enough for this task, you can put the brine in a cooler and use that instead, though you'll need to add ice to the solution along the way.

─────────── A SIMPLE BRINE ───────────

¾ cup plus 2 tablespoons kosher salt
¾ cup sugar
1 carrot, peeled and diced
1 large onion, peeled and diced
¼ cup diced celery
2 bay leaves
1 tablespoon black peppercorns
¼ teaspoon red pepper flakes
¼ teaspoon fennel seeds
2 or 3 sprigs fresh thyme

1. In the largest stockpot you can lay your hands on, bring 2 gallons of water to a boil. Add salt and sugar, and stir until dissolved.

2. Turn off heat and add carrot, onion, and celery. Add bay leaves, peppercorns, red pepper flakes, fennel seeds, and thyme. Take off heat and refrigerate until cold. Submerge turkey in brine and refrigerate for up to 72 hours.

HOW LONG WILL THE TURKEY TAKE TO COOK?

IN AN OVEN SET to 325 degrees, a whole turkey will roast at approximately 15 minutes per pound. Do not trust those plastic pop-up thermometers that are inserted in some turkeys, even free-range organic ones with college diplomas. Get a good-quality, battery-powered digital thermometer with an oven-safe probe. These are not terribly expensive, certainly in comparison to an overdone turkey, and will change your cooking life for the better for years to come.

When the number at the thigh hits 165 degrees, pull the bird from the oven and tent it under aluminum foil for at least 30 minutes to rest.

GUIDELINES

12- to 16-pound turkey: roughly 4 hours.
16- to 20-pound turkey: roughly 5 hours.
20- to 26-pound turkey: 6 hours or more.

In addition to using this chart and a thermometer, there are ways to tell that a turkey has completed its roasting. There should be at least a cup of juice in the bottom of the pan in addition to the fat that has run off the skin. The meat at the thickest part of the leg should feel fairly tender. And a wiggle of the drumstick should suggest a bone that is loose in the bird's hip socket, eager to be yanked off and chewed.

TURKEY TERMS AND TYPES

WHAT KIND OF TURKEY should you buy for Thanksgiving? The options are dizzying.

Frozen Supermarket Turkey

THE ARCHETYPE THANKSGIVING PROTEIN is a frozen turkey purchased from the supermarket. Maybe this turkey grew up in paradise and was dispatched with love. More likely, however, the bird was raised and processed on a crowded factory farm, bred to grow into adulthood as quickly as possible, and fed antibiotics to keep it healthy along the way. Flash-frozen to o degrees, it may have been warehoused for some time in advance of the Thanksgiving holiday.

Fresh Turkey

FRESH, IN THE NOMENCLATURE of poultry sales, means unfrozen—it denotes a bird that has been brought right to the edge of frozen, without the flesh going solid in the cold. You will find fresh turkeys in butcher shops and farmer's markets—they are often the sort of birds that you need to call in advance to reserve, and that are significantly more expensive than your factory-farmed frozen bird. For the administration of a proper Thanksgiving, a fresh turkey is generally the bird that you want: it is more likely, though by no means is it guaranteed, that a fresh turkey will have better flavor than his cousin deep in the supermarket freezer bin.

Kosher Turkey

KOSHER TURKEYS ARE FREE-RANGE, grain-fed birds whose processing is supervised by a rabbi, which leads to some additional cost to the consumer. They receive no antibiotics along the way from birth to death. Because they are salted as part of the koshering process, a kind of dry brine, they generally provide juicy meat. And proving that there is no rule without an exception, a frozen kosher turkey is no terrible thing to buy, so long as you allow enough time for the meat to thaw.

Free-Range Turkey

A FREE-RANGE TURKEY CONJURES images of birds frolicking in open fields. That is not the case. Free-range, in the matter of poultry, means that the birds are shunted out of their pens into an open common area for a certain number of minutes a day, where they court illness before returning to their feed. That feed may or may not contain antibiotics. A free-range bird will probably taste better than a non-free-range bird. But the adjective is not the reason: "free-range" is a marketing term that has little to do with the quality or flavor of the meat it describes. Look for the adjective in conjunction with another: a free-range kosher turkey, for instance, or a free-range organic one.

Organic Turkey

AN ORGANIC TURKEY IS a turkey that has not been treated with antibiotics, and that has eaten only feed that was itself grown organically, with no chemical processing. The label is not in itself a guarantee of better taste. But as with a free-range turkey, there are good odds an organic one will taste better than the frozen old toms they hand out for free at the local used-car lot.

Heritage Turkey

THE MOST COMMON COMMERCIAL strain of turkey in the United States is the Broad Breasted White. It could hardly exist in nature. Its huge chest and relatively tiny legs combine to create a situation in which it cannot breed without human assistance. (Sounds delicious, no?) Increasingly, however, farmers are breeding older "heritage" strains of turkey—Bourbon Reds, Narragansetts, and Bronzes among them—that recall the shape and flavors of turkeys that our forebears consumed. These are leaner birds, in the main, with more dark leg and thigh meat and correspondingly less breast meat than their more popular cousins. They take well to brine, and make for an excellent Thanksgiving centerpiece.

SOME WORDS ON THAWING
FROZEN TURKEYS

ONE OF THE MOST common questions I received in my role as the Thanksgiving help-desk correspondent for *The New York Times* is what to do with a frozen turkey. The answer on a

Thanksgiving morning is generally: not much. You can't hurry science. So plan ahead.

Guidelines

THE BEST WAY TO thaw a turkey is slowly. Place the frozen bird in the refrigerator, still in its package, breast side up, on a platter. In a refrigerator set to 40 degrees, it will defrost at a rate of approximately four pounds a day.

The second-best way to thaw a turkey is in a cold-water bath, in either the sink or a cooler. (You could use a bathtub in a pinch.) Place the frozen bird in enough cold water to cover it, and change that water frequently in order to keep it cold. It will defrost at a rate of approximately two pounds an hour.

The worst way to defrost a turkey is to leave it out on a countertop at room temperature. This method offers a fast-track route to bacterial growth and the worst Thanksgiving of your life.

TWO FAST WAYS TO ROAST TURKEY

MAYBE YOUR KITCHEN IS not big enough to handle cooking a turkey and a bunch of side dishes all at once. Perhaps the notion of roasting a turkey for five hours is crazy to you. Perhaps you simply do not have the time.

There are ways to handle this situation properly—they may even result in better, juicier meat, with more evenly browned skin.

One method is to butterfly the bird before cooking it, which the British call spatchcocking. My friend Mark Bittman, the food and opinion writer for *The New York Times*, helped popularize the technique in America.

Simply place the bird on a cutting board with its breast side down, and use a sharp knife or cleaver to cut out its backbone. (Chop this into a few pieces and use for turkey stock.) Then flatten the butterflied bird, breast side up, into a roasting pan with a few pats of sweet butter and some fresh herbs tucked into the crevices under the wings. Shower the thing with kosher salt and freshly ground black pepper, and slide it into a 450 degree oven.

A half hour later, turn the oven down to 325 degrees, baste the bird, and go sit on the couch for a little bit. The whole thing should be done in a bit over an hour.

That method takes a big roasting pan. If you only have a medium-sized one, you can go a step further, and butcher the bird entirely in advance of cooking it. The additional task of removing the legs and thighs is work your butcher can certainly do for you. But as with the removal of the backbone, it is fast work for the amateur as well.

––––––––– FASTER ROAST TURKEY –––––––––

1 12- to 18-pound turkey, thawed, with giblets and
   neck removed
1 medium onion, peeled and quartered
2 stalks celery, cleaned and roughly chopped
Fresh herbs to taste—thyme, sage, and rosemary all
   work well (optional)
3 tablespoons kosher salt
1½ tablespoons freshly ground black pepper

6 tablespoons unsalted butter, softened and cut into
   small pats

1. Preheat oven to 450 degrees. Place the turkey on a cutting board with its breast side down, and using a very sharp knife or cleaver, cut out the bird's backbone.

2. Turn the turkey over and use your knife or cleaver to remove the legs and thighs. Using cleaver, cut thighs into large chunks.

3. Press down on the turkey breasts to flatten the carcass and then, using cotton butcher's twine, truss the wings tight to the bird.

4. Place the turkey parts in one large roasting pan. Tuck between them onion, celery pieces, and, if using, herbs, and shower with salt and pepper. Dot turkey pieces with pats of butter.

5. Place pan in a 450 degree oven for 30 minutes, then reduce heat to 325 degrees and baste with accumulated juices.

6. Start to check the temperature of the breast and the thigh meat roughly 15 minutes later, and remove them from the oven when they have reached 165 degrees. As with a whole bird, you should tent the meat with foil and allow it to rest for at least 30 minutes.

HOW TO CARVE A
THANKSGIVING TURKEY

GO AHEAD. SHOW EVERYONE your finished turkey in its golden suit, allow yourself that Norman Rockwell moment as people get ready to eat. But do not ever carve your

Thanksgiving turkey at the Thanksgiving table if you can help it—and you can. Carving is an ugly business that gets messy fast. It is rarely completed without error. This is particularly the case for those who carve meats only once or twice a year. So do not court disaster. Head back into the kitchen where you can perform the surgery alone.

What you need:

A cutting board, preferably one that has some kind of reservoir routed into it so that turkey juices don't run all over the floor.

A warm platter, on which to put the carved meat.

A sharp knife, ideally a carving knife, long and thin, and a large fork or a pair of kitchen tongs to hold the meat.

A pot of steaming turkey stock on the stove, for moistening and warming the meat before it returns to the dining room.

And, finally, at least if you were raised by my mother, you will need a small bowl of finely minced parsley to sprinkle over everything before it goes out to the dining room because that is how dishes of carved poultry are meant to be served.

1. Now to the start of the knife work. Working with extreme confidence, remove one of the breast lobes, cutting in a straight line down the center of the turkey, along the bird's breast bone and wishbone, then back around through the skin. This will create a thick wedge of turkey

breast. Place it temporarily on the warmed platter. Repeat on the opposite side.

2. Cut off the drumsticks. To do so, cut skin around the legs, right where they meet the body of the bird. Grasp the end of one drumstick with one hand, and with the knife in the other, cut down into the joint between the leg and the body of the bird. Remove the leg by pulling the drumstick out and back, and using the knife to separate it from the thigh. Place drumstick on one end of the warmed platter and repeat on the other side of the bird, placing

that drumstick on the other end of the platter as a kind of framing device for the finished dish.

3. Do the same with the wings, and place these next to the legs. Now turn the turkey carcass over and remove the thighs. Slice the meat against the grain, helping to make what ought already to be tender turkey all the more so, and fan this out next to the legs and wings on the platter.

4. Return the turkey carcass to the roasting pan and cover it with foil. There is still plenty of meat on it for leftovers and picking through. But for the moment of the Thanksgiving dinner itself, it is irrelevant.

5. Take the breasts you have removed from the turkey and place these onto the cutting board. Slice these against the grain, as you did with the dark meat. Place the breast meat onto the warmed platter, and ladle a small amount of turkey stock over the top of everything to warm it up a

little. Sprinkle with the parsley if you want to please my mother, and serve.

A FEW MORE TURKEY RECIPES

WE HAVE COVERED THE fundamentals. We have roasted a whole turkey and one cut into parts. We have brined a turkey and cooked one without brine. Pair the result with gravy (pages 71–73) and some cranberry sauce (page 75), some dressing (pages 49–53) and side dishes (pages 55–67), and you have cooked Thanksgiving properly.

You are good to go, at least until the moment you decide you want to try something else.

Here are two other ways you can cook a turkey properly.

Fried Turkey

I FIRST HAD A fried turkey at a dove shoot in rural Delaware, fired up with Cajun spices and left out on a sideboard for everyone to carve for sandwiches. It was about the best thing I had ever eaten at the time, and I vowed to make one myself, as soon as I could.

That time came within a year, and if someone had filmed the process, it would have made a strong infomercial on how not to fry a turkey. I cooked with a friend, the two of us amped on beer and adrenaline, standing outside on a Brooklyn sidewalk: two city-kid rednecks with a fried-turkey rig purchased from a home improvement store, the pot filled with peanut oil, a propane hob roaring below it.

Fried turkeys cook at a blazingly fast 3½ minutes a pound when the oil is at 350 degrees. Our oil could have been running near twice that temperature. Or half. Our thermometer did not work. Whichever, we burned the turkey badly and managed somehow to pierce the bottom of the pot while doing so, igniting the oil and starting a fire that nearly engulfed a woman dressed in white Daisy Dukes who would later become my wife.

The cops came. We were pouring kitty litter onto the dying flames. One said, "Your technique needs work."

Years later, here is my best recipe for a fried turkey: a fast and furious process that results in a tightly sealed, beautifully burnished turkey of deep juiciness and shatteringly crisp skin.

The recipe gives a wide berth to brining. (Also to stuffing, for the obvious reason that it would absorb a great deal of oil.) I am not one of those who feel that it is necessary to brine a bird that is so tightly sealed by the cooking process. Moreover, I believe the process of frying a brined bird dangerous, though certainly it can be done. If you are not exceedingly careful, the excess moisture within the turkey can be converted too quickly in the frying pot to steam, which (true story!) blows the breasts right off the carcass in the hot oil and creates all kinds of issues you don't want to deal with on Thanksgiving, or any other day.

Whether to brine a turkey you intend to fry should depend on your experience with the process and the kind of bird you are frying.

More advice: Most fried-turkey kits (cooking hob, giant pot, rack for the bird) come with a large syringe that some use to inject the meat with marinade in advance of the frying. Pass on this. The risks (a bolus of marinade in the breast, pierced skin, etc.) far outweigh the reward.

Finally, and one hopes obviously: Cook outdoors on a plot of land you do not mind desecrating with hot oil if things start to splatter or problems arise. Make sure you are a good distance from your house or any other structure, so that you do not become a feature on the evening news if something goes really, terribly wrong.

Make sure, also, that you have a long-pronged candy thermometer in the oil, so that you know what temperature it is while you are cooking. And wear shoes!

DEEP-FRIED TURKEY

1 12- to 16-pound turkey, thawed, with giblets and
*   neck removed*
3 tablespoons kosher salt
1½ tablespoons freshly ground black pepper
2 teaspoons cayenne pepper, or to taste
1 5-gallon container peanut oil

1. Place the turkey in an empty fryer pot and cover with water. Remove the turkey from the pot, rinse, and dry with paper towels. Mark the water level with a marker on the outside of the pot, or score the inside with a nail or paring knife. You will need that much oil in the pot when you cook, and no more. Empty the pot, then wash and dry.

2. Rub the bird inside and out with salt, pepper, and cayenne.

3. Fill pot with peanut oil so that it reaches the level the water was after the turkey was removed, and attach an extra-long candy thermometer to the inside of the pot. Heat oil over an outdoor propane hob until the oil reaches 350 degrees.

4. Meanwhile, place the turkey on its rack—generally a device shaped something like a grappling hook, with a long shank, that will allow you to put the bird into the heated oil and re-

trieve it at the end of the cooking process. Simply thread the bird onto the shank so that it sits with its breast side up.

5. Working carefully, use the handle that attaches to the rack to lower the turkey slowly into the heated oil. The process may take up to a minute, as the oil bubbles and pops because of excess moisture on the exterior of the bird. Wear gloves, and do not perform your duties barefoot or while drunk.

6. Cook for approximately 3½ minutes per pound. Remove from oil, allowing the excess to drain off the carcass, and allow the bird to rest for at least 30 minutes, covered in foil. Remove bird from rack and carve.

Grilled Turkey

GRILLING A TURKEY FOR Thanksgiving is one of the great dark arts of holiday cooking.

It is an excellent choice for those who wish to spend much of the day outside, tending to fires and keeping away from family. Requiring only patience, good humor, and knowledge of a few rules, grilling can lead to a meal that is rather more rustic in flavor than the average Thanksgiving, but no less delicious and sometimes quite a bit more.

I have cooked Thanksgiving turkeys on gas grills, using little foil packets of wood chips to create the necessary smoke. You can do so as well. But I find the experience roughly equivalent to cooking a turkey in a small, drafty oven, and the results are no match for those that occur when the bird is roasted in the presence of a glowing charcoal fire.

What you want instead is a covered charcoal grill that is large enough that there can be a small fire on one side of the grate and the turkey on the other, with good charcoal—the sort that is not impregnated with lighter fluid—and wood chips of the sort that flavor meat without turning it acrid: oak is nice, or cherry, or apple, or hickory—green hickory if you can find it. (The best smoked turkey I have ever eaten, at Mac's barbecue shop in Deep Ellum, in Dallas, was cooked over the smoke of just that wood.)

Avoid any soft wood with a lot of pitch. Once I smoke-roasted a Thanksgiving turkey over pine, thinking it might be delicious. It tasted like an ashtray.

Two notes: First, using a brine beforehand is a good way to help ensure that the bird remains juicy during the long cooking process—opportunities for basting are few and far between in the world of the grilled turkey.

Second, do not stuff the bird. The results are grim from both a culinary standpoint and, potentially, a health-safety one, since the process generally takes longer than in a conventional oven, and the dressing will be at a dangerously low temperature for hours.

——— SMOKE-ROASTED TURKEY ———

1 12- to 16-pound turkey, thawed, with giblets and
   neck removed, brined (page 30)
2 tablespoons unsalted butter, softened
3 tablespoons kosher salt
1½ tablespoons freshly ground black pepper
2 apples, cored and cut into quarters
2 oranges, cut into quarters
1 red onion, peeled and cut into quarters

1. Place a large disposable aluminum roasting pan with a few cups of water in it in the bottom of your charcoal grill, and build a small charcoal fire around it, using roughly a shoebox-sized portion of briquettes.

2. Rinse turkey and dry carefully with paper towels. Rub the bird inside and out with butter and salt and pepper. Place the apples, oranges, and onion in the cavity of the bird, and bind the drumsticks together with butcher's twine.

3. When the fire has died down and the coals are covered with ash, place the turkey directly above the drip pan, making sure that no part of the bird is over a burning coal. Cover the grill, crack open the vents in the cover about ⅛ inch, and cook, adding a handful of charcoal or wood chips every 30 minutes or so.

4. As in a conventional oven, the turkey will cook at approximately 15 minutes per pound—though if you're not careful with heat management, the time will be closer to 20 minutes per pound. (Turn the bird a few times on the grill to ensure even browning.) After a few hours, insert a meat thermometer straight down into fleshiest part of thigh, where it meets the drumstick, and check the temperature. Do not let the thermometer touch the bone. The turkey is done when the thigh meat reaches 165 degrees, with juices running clear when you remove the thermometer.

5. When bird has reached desired temperature, remove from grill and let rest for at least 30 minutes, covered in foil. Remove foil and carve.

CHAPTER THREE

SIDE DISHES

O NE OF THE FIRST things I learned as a Thanksgiving help-line reporter at *The New York Times* was how set in their ways people can be about holiday side dishes. Every year questions poured in about oven temperatures for turkeys, about how to make desserts, about whether a cranberry sauce was going to gel. But rare was the query about whipping better mashed potatoes or how to glaze carrots. How to make better side dishes? No one seemed to want to know these things.

There were debates about which is more important: the bird or the side dishes. These will go on forever, more than a little because the two cannot live without each other. A Thanksgiving meal devoid of sides or of turkey would be no Thanksgiving at all. But even as we struggle to come up with new recipes for our turkeys and our desserts, it is fascinating the degree to which we stick to our faithful ones for side dishes, how when it comes to cooking these platters we are so resistant to change.

In some respects this resistance is understandable, and important. We honor our forebears by making the food they taught us to make—Aunt Ethel's marshmallow-dotted sweet potatoes, say, or Mom's barbecued beans. (My father's creamed Brussels sprouts appear on page 63.) But in other important ways we are missing out. As we know from our experimentation with turkeys, the arrival of new flavors on Thanksgiving plates offers the possibility of new traditions and, with them, new outlooks on the holiday.

As always there are rules for this sort of exploration. One is, do not cook outside the season. It is of no matter that somewhere on the planet an industrialist has figured out how to farm asparagus year-round. Asparagus is a spring vegetable and has no place on the fall holiday table. (As a corollary, there is no place for marshmallows either, unless you have had marshmallows on your Thanksgiving table since childhood.)

Instead, keep your attentions on gourds and tubers, on the end of the growing season, on things to which you can add butter and cream, maple syrup and bacon.

Moreover, you should offer more than one starch to the Thanksgiving table, and more than one vegetable. This is both in the interest of variety and in celebration of the excess called for by the holiday. What is Thanksgiving, after all, without plates utterly crowded with colors and textures and tastes?

But as I have said and will say again: you should make no salad. And you should cook no appetizers, whether you call them side dishes or not. I have tested this rage, so that you do not need to: nothing is more annoying at Thanksgiving than spending an entire day cooking for people only to see them crush their hunger an hour before dinner by inhaling a pound of cheese, olives, or deviled eggs. Nothing is grimmer than seeing someone forgo a second plate of dressing and thigh meat and yams and Brussels sprouts in the name of a thatch of arugula dressed with nuts and cheese, slicked down with olive oil.

———— FRESH BREAD DRESSING ————

It is dressing because it is cooked outside of the bird. Placed within the cavity of a bird, it becomes stuffing. This recipe is appropriate almost year-round as an accompaniment to roast chicken or pork chops.

5 tablespoons unsalted butter
1 large Spanish onion, peeled and diced
2 stalks celery, cleaned and diced
2 apples, preferably tart (like Granny Smith or Cortland), peeled, cored, and diced
Kosher salt and freshly ground black pepper to taste
8 to 10 fresh sage leaves, rolled together and sliced thin
2 sprigs fresh thyme, chopped
1 dash hot pepper sauce, or to taste
1 loaf French or Italian bread, torn into small pieces
½ cup to 1 cup turkey stock (page 19) or chicken stock (if using store-bought, use low-sodium variety)
1 egg, beaten
½ cup chopped parsley

1. Melt 4 tablespoons of the butter in a large skillet set over medium heat. Add onion, celery, apples, salt, pepper, sage,

thyme, and hot pepper sauce. Cook, stirring, until vegetables have softened and herbs wilted, approximately 5 minutes.

2. Transfer mixture to a large bowl. Add the bread, beaten egg, parsley, and enough stock to make the dressing moist but not wet. Blend well and check for seasoning.

3. Grease a medium-sized baking dish with the remaining 1 tablespoon butter and put dressing in it. Bake, uncovered, for 30 minutes or until the top is beginning to brown. Check to make sure interior is moist. If not, add some more stock and return to oven for 5 to 10 minutes longer.

THREE-PEPPER SAUSAGE CORNBREAD DRESSING

Here is a recipe I adapted from the cooking of Kurt Gardner, a New York theater man of great culinary passions who has been contributing the dish to our home for years, usually in proportions large enough to feed boroughs. Rare is the month where there is not a frozen bag of this stuff in our freezer, ready to be deployed.

2 tablespoons extra-virgin olive oil

1½ pounds andouille sausage, or fresh chorizo or hot Italian sausage

1 medium yellow onion, peeled and diced

2 stalks celery, cleaned and diced

2 red or orange bell peppers, cored, seeded, and diced

2 poblano or Anaheim peppers, seeded and diced

2 serrano or jalapeño peppers, seeded and diced

2 tablespoons fresh cilantro, cleaned and roughly chopped

Kosher salt and freshly ground black pepper to taste
2 cups chicken stock (if using store-bought, use low-sodium variety)
1 pan cornbread, cut into cubes (recipe follows)

1. Preheat oven to 375 degrees.

2. Heat olive oil in large flat-bottomed sauté pan over medium-high heat. Add sausage and sauté until browned, approximately 10 minutes. Remove to a large bowl and set aside.

3. Add onion to the pan and reduce heat to medium, then sauté until onion begins to turn clear and soften, approximately 5 minutes. Add celery and peppers and continue cooking until peppers begin to soften, approximately 10 minutes.

4. Pour vegetable mixture into bowl with sausage, add chopped cilantro, salt and pepper to taste, and toss to mix.

5. Return pan to heat and deglaze with a splash of chicken stock, then scrape contents into bowl with sausage and vegetable mixture.

6. Pour mixture into a large roasting pan and add cubed cornbread, mixing by hand. Add chicken stock to moisten, cover with aluminum foil, and place in oven for 30 to 35 minutes, or until it is soft and the flavors well incorporated. If you desire a crunchy top, remove foil for final 10 minutes of cooking. (Dressing can be made ahead of time and reheated when needed. If dry upon reheating, add additional chicken stock.)

CORNBREAD

John Willoughby, once the executive editor of *Gourmet* and, with the chef Chris Schlesinger, one of the great interpreters of live-fire cooking in the United States, once said that there are only 11 recipes in the world, and those of us who labor in kitchens spend most of our time reinventing them.

As an example, here is my adaptation of the recipe for cornbread Schlesinger served in his East Coast Grill from the time he opened the place in Cambridge, Massachusetts, in 1985 to when he sold it in 2012. The adaptation? I have added a few cups of frozen organic corn for texture. Those who wish to go further might add a fine dice of fiery chipotle peppers in adobo sauce, or cook a few slices of bacon in the skillet before cooking the dish, and add the crumbled result to the batter. The fat left over in the pan would allow you to reduce the amount of butter you use by about 2 tablespoons.

> *4 cups all-purpose flour*
> *2 cups yellow cornmeal*
> *1½ cups sugar*
> *1 teaspoon kosher salt*
> *2 tablespoons baking powder*
> *4 large eggs*
> *3 cups whole milk*
> *2½ tablespoons vegetable oil*
> *1 10-ounce package frozen organic corn kernels*
> *8 tablespoons unsalted butter, melted*

1. Preheat oven to 350 degrees. Lightly oil a 9-inch cast-iron skillet or a 12 by 8 by 2-inch pan, and place it in the oven to heat.

2. In a large bowl, sift together the flour, cornmeal, sugar, salt, and baking powder. In a separate bowl, whisk together the eggs, milk, and oil. Pour the wet ingredients over the dry ingre-

dients, add the corn, and stir until just combined. Add the butter and stir once or twice to incorporate.

3. Remove the hot skillet or pan from the oven, pour batter into it, and give the whole number a smack on the counter to settle it. Put pan in oven to cook until mixture is brown on top and a sharp knife inserted into its center comes out clean, approximately 1 hour. Cornbread can, indeed should, be made ahead of time. If it is slightly stale at the start of the process, so much the better—the dried cornbread leads to a fluffier dressing.

GIBLET, CHESTNUT, AND OYSTER DRESSING

This is professional-grade-project dressing, made easier if you can find peeled chestnuts in the market or online. (Which you can!) Bottled or canned oysters may likewise be substituted for the freshly shucked, but that would begin to move matters in a direction I would characterize as incorrect. There should be very little that is prepackaged about Thanksgiving. As this dish shows, hard work can pay off in big flavors and fantastic textures, a dressing for the ages.

½ pound fresh chestnuts
Turkey giblets—the gizzard and heart from 1 bird
1 dozen fresh oysters, shucked and kept with their
   liquor (approximately 1 cup)
8 tablespoons unsalted butter
1 large Spanish onion, peeled and chopped
2 stalks celery, cleaned and chopped

1 tablespoon finely chopped fresh sage
1 tablespoon finely chopped fresh thyme
2 tablespoons chopped parsley
6 cups pieces of stale bread (in bits about the size of
   dice or soda-bottle caps)
½ cup turkey stock (page 19) or chicken stock
Kosher salt and freshly ground black pepper to taste

1. To peel chestnuts, cut deep X's into the flat side of the nuts. Place them in a pot of well-salted water, bring to a boil over high heat, then reduce heat and simmer for about 15 minutes. Drain the pot, cover the nuts with lukewarm water, and allow to cool slightly. Then, using a paring knife, peel away the outer shell and inner skin of each chestnut. It sounds easy. It is not.

2. In a small pot over medium heat, combine giblets with enough water to cover them and simmer for 30 minutes or so, until tender. Remove giblets from water and chop into small pieces.

3. Preheat oven to 350 degrees. In a small pot set over medium heat, gently poach oysters in their own liquid for approximately 5 minutes, then remove from heat and chop into small pieces.

4. Melt 6 tablespoons of the butter in a large skillet set over medium heat. Add onion, celery, sage, thyme, and parsley. Cook, stirring, until vegetables have softened and herbs wilted, approximately 5 minutes.

5. Transfer mixture to a large bowl. Add the bread pieces, giblets, chestnuts, and oysters. Blend well, and add enough oyster liquor or stock to moisten the whole, and check for seasoning.

6. Grease a large baking dish with the remaining 2 tablespoons butter and put dressing in it. Bake, uncovered, for 30 minutes or until the top is beginning to brown. Check to make sure interior is moist. If not, add some more stock and return to oven for 5 to 10 minutes longer.

MASHED POTATOES

You can make mashed potatoes lumpy with a fork or a masher device, or smooth with a food mill or a stand mixer. And of course you can make them without peeling the potatoes, if you scrub the skins well. This makes for an attractive, rustic-looking dish. Indeed, the only trouble that should ever present itself when the subject comes to mashed potatoes and Thanksgiving is should someone demand that garlic or basil be added to the mix. Your response to this heresy should be brief and unequivocal: No. This is Thanksgiving. There is no place in the holiday for a mixture of garlic and potatoes, much less basil and potatoes. The flavors clash with the turkey and the other sides. No.

2 pounds potatoes, ideally organic Yukon Golds,
though an Idaho or Russet will do well, peeled and
cut into quarters
4 tablespoons unsalted butter
¾ cup whole milk, warmed but not boiling
Kosher salt and freshly ground black pepper

1. Place the potatoes in a large, heavy-bottomed pot and cover them with water. Set the pot over high heat and boil the potatoes until soft, approximately 30 minutes.

2. Drain potatoes and shake to remove as much water as possible, then mash them or use a stand mixer to whip them. Return to pot, place over very low heat, and add butter in pats, stirring slowly with a wooden spoon. Add warmed milk gradually and continue to beat until the dish is to your liking. Season to taste with salt and pepper. Serve in a warmed bowl.

SCALLOPED POTATOES

Here is an elegant alternative to mashed potatoes, which you can make a day or so ahead of time, store in the refrigerator, and easily reheat under foil in a 350 degree oven for 20 or 25 minutes. The preparation is slightly French (and there is even some garlic!), but the nutmeg gives the starch a fine American accent. Those interested in a slightly heavier version might consider the addition of ham or cooked bacon, layered in amid the potatoes and cream.

1½ cups whole milk
½ cup cream
1 large clove garlic, peeled, smashed, and minced
½ teaspoon freshly grated nutmeg
Kosher salt and ground white pepper, or freshly ground
*   black pepper, to taste*
2 pounds Yukon Gold potatoes, peeled, sliced thin, and
*   kept in a bowl of cold water*
3 tablespoons unsalted butter

1. Preheat oven to 425 degrees. Combine milk and cream in a small saucepan and bring to almost a boil. Remove from heat and add garlic, nutmeg, salt, and pepper. Set aside.

2. Lightly butter a 9-inch square baking dish or 9-inch casserole with half of the butter. Drain the potatoes and dry them lightly, then layer half of them in the dish so that they overlap slightly. Add half the milk, pouring it all over the potatoes. Layer the remainder of the potatoes in the dish, then add the rest of the milk so that it comes almost to their top.

3. Top with dots of the rest of the butter and place in the upper third of the oven until the potatoes are browned and the milk has been absorbed, 45 minutes to 1 hour. Serve in its container.

MASHED AND SLIGHTLY SPICY SWEET POTATOES

This is my take on an old Bobby Flay recipe, presumably based in part on the color of his hair. It capitalizes on the sauce left over from the can of chipotles in adobo sauce that seems always to sit in the back of my refrigerator. You can increase the spiciness by adding more chipotle, and dial down the sweetness by reducing the amount of maple syrup. A fancy cat would use crème fraîche instead of sour cream. That would be totally acceptable.

5 pounds (about 10 medium or 5 large) sweet potatoes, scrubbed
⅓ cup best-quality maple syrup
¾ cup sour cream
4 teaspoons sauce from canned chipotles
1½ teaspoons ground cinnamon
Kosher salt to taste

1. Put oven rack in middle position and preheat oven to 375 degrees. Place potatoes on a large baking sheet and bake until soft, 35 to 40 minutes for medium potatoes, up to 1 hour for large.

2. Meanwhile, in a small bowl, whisk together the syrup, sour cream, chipotle sauce, cinnamon, and salt.

3. When potatoes are very tender, remove from oven and slice in half lengthwise. Scoop the flesh into a potato ricer, food mill, or stand mixer and process into a purée. Add other ingredients and stir with a rubber spatula to combine. Potatoes should be light and fluffy. Taste for seasoning and serve in a warmed bowl.

—— ROASTED BUTTERNUT SQUASH ——
WITH BUTTER AND SAGE

Here is one of those recipes that may lead people to wonder why it is they don't eat butternut squash throughout the year. The butter and sage interact with the flesh of the vegetable in satisfying, marvelous ways, and the combination makes a perfect foil for bird and gravy, for dressing and greens.

> *2 tablespoons extra-virgin olive oil*
> *2 large butternut squash, halved lengthwise and seeded*
> *8 tablespoons unsalted butter*
> *8 to 10 fresh sage leaves, rolled together and sliced thin*
> *Kosher salt and freshly ground black pepper*

1. Preheat oven to 400 degrees. Rub a large baking sheet and the cut sides of the squash with oil and place the squash cut side

down on the sheet. Place in oven and roast until very tender, 50 to 60 minutes.

2. Meanwhile, melt butter in a small saucepan set over medium heat. Add sage and cook, swirling the mixture occasionally, until butter is golden in hue. The sage will be fairly crisp at this point. Remove from heat.

3. Remove squash from oven, turn over, and cut pieces into even thirds. Place on a warmed platter, season to taste with salt and pepper, drizzle with the butter, sprinkle with the sage, and serve.

—— STEAMED BUTTERNUT SQUASH —— WITH BUTTER AND PARSLEY

This is a very, very easy recipe—just so long as you do not scorch the squash while you are braising it on the stovetop. So be mindful. Instructions are not guarantees—they are signposts. If in doubt, you can always add a little more butter.

2 large butternut squash, halved lengthwise, seeded,
*   peeled, and cut into large bite-sized cubes*
4 tablespoons unsalted butter
2 tablespoons chopped parsley
Kosher salt and freshly ground black pepper

1. Place squash in a large saucepan with a cover, and fill with just enough water to come halfway up the squash. Add half the butter and place over high heat until water comes to a boil. Stir once or twice and cover the pan, reducing heat to medium.

Cook until the squash is tender, approximately 10 minutes, adding a little more liquid if needed.

2. Remove top, add the rest of the butter, and stir to glaze the squash. Sprinkle with parsley, season to taste with salt and pepper, and serve.

—— ROASTED CAULIFLOWER WITH —— ANCHOVY BREAD CRUMBS

It is important to note that this dish does not have an anchovy flavor. Indeed, there is no reason ever to tell anyone who eats this dish that there are anchovies in it. The taste is merely salty and rich—and reflects beautifully off the sweet, creamy taste of the cauliflower beneath its slightly crunchy bread crumb topping.

2 heads cauliflower
8 to 10 fresh sage leaves, roughly chopped
Zest of 2 lemons
2 teaspoons sugar
2 tablespoons extra-virgin olive oil
Kosher salt and freshly ground black pepper to taste

For the anchovy bread crumbs

¼ cup extra-virgin olive oil
8 anchovy fillets, rinsed and finely chopped
3 cloves garlic, peeled and finely chopped

1 shallot, peeled and diced
1 cup fresh bread crumbs

1. Preheat oven to 400 degrees. Break cauliflower into florets and toss in a bowl with sage, lemon zest, sugar, and olive oil. Season with salt and pepper and spread out on a large baking sheet. Place in oven and cook until tender and golden, approximately 20 to 25 minutes.

2. Meanwhile, prepare bread crumbs. Heat olive oil in a sauté pan set over medium heat. When oil shimmers, add the anchovies, garlic, shallot, and bread crumbs. Cook for 5 to 7 minutes, until golden.

3. In a large bowl, toss together cauliflower and bread crumbs and serve on a warmed platter.

—————— BASIC GREEN BEANS ——————

Another simple recipe you might make a dozen times each year. When you bore of it, throw in some changeups: sliced and butter-toasted almonds, say, or pancetta and mint. Indeed, either of these variations would be entirely correct to serve at Thanksgiving. But first, the basics.

2 pounds fresh green beans, tailed and topped
2 teaspoons lemon juice, white wine, or zest of
  1 lemon
3 tablespoons unsalted butter, melted
Kosher salt and freshly ground black pepper to taste

1. Bring a large pot filled with salted water to a rolling boil over high heat. Add green beans and cook for 3 to 4 minutes, or until they are bright green and as tender as you like.

2. Drain beans and toss with lemon and butter. Adjust seasonings. Serve in a warmed bowl.

―――― SLOW-COOKED GREEN BEANS ――――

Those thinking of frying a turkey for the holiday, or of steering the meal in any southward direction, should consider this simple, delicious take on a staple of the Southern cafeteria circuit: slow-simmered green beans in a smoky turkey stock. Save that liquor when you are done cooking the beans. It will enliven whatever soup or pot of beans you add it to in future.

> *4 tablespoons unsalted butter or bacon fat*
> *1 large Spanish onion, peeled and chopped*
> *2 pounds fresh green beans, tailed and topped*
> *1 smoked turkey neck or leg or wing*
> *Kosher salt and freshly ground black pepper to*
>   *taste*

1. Put butter in a large, heavy pot over medium-high heat and allow it to melt. When it foams, add onion and cook, stirring frequently, until it softens and begins to go slack.

2. Add green beans, smoked turkey, a sprinkle of salt, and a grind or two of pepper, and cover with water—approximately 5 cups. Turn heat to high and bring pot to a boil.

3. Reduce heat and allow pot to simmer, stirring occasionally, until beans are very tender and dense, 50 to 60 minutes.

Strain beans, retaining liquor for another use, and discard turkey part. Serve beans.

—— CREAMED BRUSSELS SPROUTS ——

Thanksgiving is not a day to consider healthful eating. This dish explains why, in a pool of thick milk and cream that is used as a kind of braising liquid and glaze combined, with bacon providing a hit of salt and smoke against the sweet of the sprouts. It is a strong bet against those who declare that they have never, ever liked Brussels sprouts. It wins hearts and minds. It was my father's annual contribution to my Thanksgiving table until his death in 2009. Now it is mine.

> *2 pounds Brussels sprouts, washed and trimmed (cut*
> *   larger ones in half)*
> *3 thick slices slab bacon or guanciale, diced*
> *1 cup light cream*
> *1 teaspoon kosher salt*
> *½ teaspoon freshly ground black pepper*
> *¼ teaspoon freshly grated nutmeg*

1. Trim the Brussels sprouts of any loose or yellowing leaves and cut a light X in the stem end of each one. Place in a quart of boiling water and cook for 5 to 7 minutes. Remove from heat, drain, and run under cold water or place in large ice bath.

2. Meanwhile, heat a large sauté pan over medium heat and add the bacon or guanciale, then allow its fat to render.

3. In a separate saucepan, heat the cream, adding to it the salt, pepper, and nutmeg. When the meat is almost crispy, add the Brussels sprouts to the pan and toss to coat with fat. Cook for 3 to 5 minutes and then add the seasoned cream. Cook for an additional few minutes, stirring frequently to coat the sprouts, until the sauce is slightly thickened. Adjust seasonings and serve immediately.

— BRAISED BRUSSELS SPROUTS WITH — BUTTERED BREAD CRUMBS

This recipe is an adaptation of dishes I've cooked over the years from two of my favorite cooks, Suzanne Goin of Lucques, in Los Angeles (among many other pursuits), and Amanda Hesser, of Food52.com (among many other pursuits). Amanda's recipe was based on a dish that appears sometimes on fall menus at Lucques. Mine is based on hers. Around and around we spin.

> *1½ cups fresh bread crumbs*
> *1 tablespoon fresh thyme leaves*
> *6 tablespoons extra-virgin olive oil*
> *4 tablespoons unsalted butter*
> *2 pounds Brussels sprouts, washed and trimmed*
> *Kosher salt and freshly ground black pepper*
> *½ pound bacon, cut into small pieces*
> *2 large shallots, peeled and minced*
> *4 cloves garlic, peeled and minced*
> *Red pepper flakes to taste (optional)*
> *½ cup cider vinegar*

½ cup turkey stock (page 19) or chicken stock (ideally
homemade) and more if needed
2 tablespoons chopped parsley

1. In a bowl, mix bread crumbs and thyme with 4 table-spoons olive oil. Pour crumbs into a large sauté pan set over medium-high heat and toast, tossing frequently, until golden brown, approximately 10 to 12 minutes. Set aside.

2. Heat butter and remaining olive oil in another large sauté pan over medium-high heat until the butter begins to foam. Add Brussels sprouts, and cook, tossing frequently, until the vegetables are lightly browned, about 5 to 7 minutes. Season with salt and pepper, then add diced bacon, and sauté, tossing frequently, until sprouts are well browned and softened slightly, and bacon is crisp, 8 to 10 minutes more. Reduce heat, add shallots and garlic, and toss until fragrant, approximately 2 to 3 minutes. Add red pepper flakes, if using.

3. Increase heat to high, add the vinegar and stock, and cook, tossing frequently, until the sprouts are glazed and tender, adding more stock if needed. Taste and adjust seasoning. Sprinkle with chopped parsley. Transfer to a serving bowl or platter and scatter the bread crumbs on top.

MAPLE-GLAZED CARROTS WITH BLACK PEPPER

I learned to cook these on a woodstove in a kitchen with no electricity or running water, and often cooked them well past the point of glazing, right into scorched and smoky. That is no terrible thing, but be careful all the same. Allow the black pepper to provide counterbalance to the sweet of the syrup and the carrots themselves.

10 carrots of decent size, peeled and cut into large pieces
4 tablespoons unsalted butter
1½ teaspoons maple syrup
1½ teaspoons freshly ground black pepper, or to taste
Kosher salt to taste

1. Place carrots in a large saucepan with a cover, and fill with just enough water to come halfway up the carrots. Add half the butter and place over high heat until it comes to a boil. Swirl the pan once or twice and cover, then reduce heat to medium. Cook until the carrots are tender, approximately 10 minutes.

2. Remove cover, add the rest of the butter, the maple syrup, and black pepper and stir to glaze the carrots. Cook for approximately 5 minutes, swirling the pan often, until carrots begin to color. Taste and adjust seasonings. Transfer to a warmed platter to serve.

MACARONI AND CHEESE

Again with the South! One of the great upsides of cooking Thanksgiving for family and friends is that the latter group will always challenge the cultural primacy of the former. You need not listen, but occasionally you ought to—especially if you grew up without macaroni and cheese on your Thanksgiving table. This one, simple and cheesey, with a good helping of crust and no white sauce to gum it up, calls for a mixture of extra-sharp Cheddar and Swiss. You might swap out the Swiss for sharp Cheddar or smoked Gouda.

2 tablespoons unsalted butter
12 ounces extra-sharp Cheddar cheese, coarsely grated
12 ounces Swiss cheese, coarsely grated
1 pound elbow pasta, boiled until just cooked,
    drained, and rinsed under cold water
1 pinch cayenne pepper or red pepper flakes (optional)
Kosher salt
⅔ cup whole milk

1. Heat oven to 375 degrees. Use butter to grease, heavily, a medium-sized baking dish. Combine cheeses and set aside at least 2 handfuls for topping.

2. In a large bowl, toss together pasta, cheese, cayenne or red pepper flakes (if using), and salt to taste. Place in pan and pour milk over the surface. Sprinkle reserved cheese on top and bake, uncovered, for 45 minutes, until bubbly. If desired, transfer to top rack of oven for final 10 to 15 minutes to brown the top.

CHAPTER FOUR

GRAVY &
CRANBERRY SAUCE

I'LL RISK STARTING A brushfire by saying with great confidence that the two most important factors in any credible Thanksgiving feast are the cranberry sauce and the gravy. Debate that all you like. But they tie every element on the plate together. They act as frame and foundation alike. And if the cranberry sauce only enhances what is already excellent, good gravy can cure almost any Thanksgiving ill. As Sammy Cahn wrote for Sinatra to sing, "You can't have one without the other."

GRAVY

THIN GRAVY IS UNACCEPTABLE. So, too, flavorless gravy, gummy gravy, too-salty gravy, gravy made with anything that comes in a foil packet—any gravy that people pass on in favor of plain, unadorned turkey meat and starch. Good gravy is what you are after here. Making it is a process that sits at the heart of cooking Thanksgiving correctly.

So how to do it?

For gravy, you must always start with the drippings left at the bottom of your roasting pan when you cook the turkey—all the gunk that's gone sticky and rich with flavor. This stuff is what chefs and fancy-food people call fond. Many recipes will tell you to get rid of excess fat in the pan before messing with the fond. And you should get rid of some of it. But not too much. (More on this below.) You want to make a lot of gravy. You need a lot of fat.

Confidence is everything. Those who believe their gravy will turn out well will turn out good gravy. The fond will help in this regard. So will the fat. And what salt you may add at the end. Work slowly, with deliberation, as if raking the lawn for a good neighbor, tasting all the way.

The turkey is out of the oven and sitting on a cutting board below its tinfoil hat, resting, with its clear-flowing juices retreating into its tender flesh. The table is set and the side dishes hot and ready to go.

This is gravy time. Take the roasting pan and place it on the stovetop, where it may cover two burners. Put one or both of these on low and allow the fat in the pan to get hot. Now sprinkle flour over its top in roughly a 1:1 ratio: a tablespoon of flour to every tablespoon of fat. I stir this stuff down with a wooden spoon, I scrape at the crusty bits, I try to get as much funk and flavor into it as possible, and I continue to stir, allowing the fat to come into the flour, to become one with it.

What kind of flour? All-purpose is fine, but if you want to stack the odds in your favor of making this gravy correctly, you should turn toward a finely milled flour, sometimes called "instant flour," like Wondra. It is more easily cut into the fat and it makes for a smoother gravy, particularly if you are just starting out in the gravy game and worried about clumps.

Let that mixture cook for a while, about 10 minutes or so, stirring it often, and allowing the raw taste of the flour to subside in the deliciousness of the fat. Then start to add warm turkey stock, slowly, a half-cup or so at a time, stirring and stirring as you do. You might find yourself holding up one end of the roasting pan and concentrating the gravy at the other. If so, turn off the heat under your holding hand.

What turkey stock? The one you made a few days before the holiday or started on Thursday morning, when you first got going on the bird. (There are recipes for stock on pages 19 and 21.) It bubbles away all day and is absolutely essential to Thanksgiving success. You can use it for gravy, or to moisten dry dressing, or to warm sliced turkey meat just before you bring it to table to serve.

The stock you add to the mixture of fat and flour will, over the course of just a few minutes, thicken into gravy, making it smooth and rich. The result should coat the back of a spoon. You might add a little cream at this point, or sherry, wine, or Cognac. Taste it for flavor. Add salt or pepper accordingly.

And that is it, at least for this basic first try. Later you can try more involved recipes, with richer stocks or the addition of giblets. You can mix and match ingredients and techniques to serve your tastes or interests. Gravy, like vinaigrette, is simply a term of art: you can do with it what you want, so long as you follow the rules.

Serve in warm bowls or gravy boats. If you are making everything ahead of time, you may cover the result and put it in the fridge, not the freezer. The gravy will turn into fragrant gelatin in the cold. But you can heat it back into perfection before serving.

PAN GRAVY

7 tablespoons turkey fat, left in roasting pan
6 tablespoons flour (ideally, instant or all-purpose)
4 to 5 cups turkey stock (page 19) or chicken stock
½ cup dry sherry
Kosher salt and freshly ground black pepper

1. Pour off all but the 7 or so tablespoons turkey fat from the pan you roasted the turkey in, and set the pan on the stovetop over medium heat. Sprinkle the flour over the fat and cook, stirring constantly, until the mixture is golden, 8 to 10 minutes.

2. Increase heat to medium high and slowly add stock, stirring constantly, until the mixture is smooth. Cook, continuing to stir, until the gravy has thickened, approximately 8 to 10 minutes. Add sherry and stir to combine. Season to taste with salt and pepper.

SERIOUS PAN GRAVY

In France, what we call gravy would be a sauce, and would derive its depth and complexity from shallots and veal stock. They are very fancy, in France. This gravy has the former, but not the latter—the turkey stock on page 19 will do. In a pinch you could even use chicken stock.

7 tablespoons turkey fat, taken from roasting pan
6 tablespoons flour (ideally, instant or all-purpose)
2 large shallots, peeled and minced
½ cup dry sherry or good white wine
4 to 5 cups serious turkey stock (page 21)
Kosher salt and freshly ground black pepper

1. Place the turkey fat in a small saucepan set over medium heat and allow to get hot. Add the flour and stir to combine, then cook, stirring constantly, until the roux is golden and smells nutty, approximately 10 minutes. Reserve.

2. Place the roasting pan with all of its sticky goodness in it on the stovetop over medium heat and allow it to get hot. Add the shallots and stir to combine, then sweat them slowly until they are soft. (If not enough fat remains in the pan after removing what you need for the roux, add a pat or two of butter instead. It's Thanksgiving!) Add the sherry or wine to deglaze the pan, and cook until only a syrup remains. Slowly add the stock, stirring, and bring to a low simmer.

3. Add the roux, a few tablespoons at a time, and whisk to combine. Stop adding roux when you have achieved the gravy consistency you desire. Season to taste with salt and pepper.

SHALLOTS VERSUS ONIONS

SHALLOTS ARE SMALLER AND more delicate in flavor and smell than their cousin the onion, and less astringent than garlic, also an allium. Named by the ancient Roman scholar Pliny, and made famous by the French, who use shallots at the base of many of their best and most flavorful sauces, they help provide a sweet, pungent base line in vinaigrettes and sautéed green beans. They are a marvelous addition to any Thanksgiving gravy, but if you cannot locate any, some finely diced onion and a scant amount of garlic will make an adequate substitution.

GIBLET GRAVY

It is best never to call giblet gravy "giblet gravy," but simply gravy. Giblets are mysterious things, terrifying to many in theory, if rarely in fact: they're just the heart and the gizzard of a bird, cooked into mineral succulence. There is no need to advertise the presence of giblets in a gravy until someone has complimented you on its flavor. Even then, it may be wise to whisper.

1 cup turkey gizzards and hearts, or chicken gizzards and hearts, or a combination
4 tablespoons unsalted butter, turkey fat, or bacon grease
7 tablespoons turkey fat, left in roasting pan
6 tablespoons flour (ideally, instant or all-purpose)

4 to 5 cups turkey stock (page 19) or chicken stock
½ cup dry sherry, white wine, or applejack
½ cup heavy cream
Kosher salt and freshly ground black pepper

1. Using a food processor or all your patience with a knife, cut the gizzards and hearts into a fine mince. Meanwhile, melt the butter in a sauté pan set over medium-high heat. When the butter has foamed, add the minced giblets and allow them to cook in the fat until they are browned and crisp, stirring occasionally, approximately 10 minutes. Remove from pan with a slotted spoon and set aside.

2. Pour off all but the 7 or so tablespoons turkey fat from the pan you roasted the turkey in, and set the pan on the stovetop over medium heat. Sprinkle the flour over the fat and cook, stirring constantly, until the mixture is golden, approximately 3 to 5 minutes.

3. Add the reserved cooked giblets and stir to combine, then increase heat to medium high, and slowly add stock, stirring constantly, until the mixture is smooth. Cook, continuing to stir, until the gravy has thickened, approximately 8 to 10 minutes. Add the sherry, wine, or applejack and stir to combine. After a minute or two, add the cream, stirring to combine and heat, then season to taste with salt and pepper.

CRANBERRY SAUCE

MAKING CRANBERRY SAUCE IS only a little more difficult than opening a can of cranberry sauce, and offers about three times the flavor and none of the high-fructose corn syrup. But I will not stand in the way of those families for whom canned cranberry sauce is a tradition—indeed, I think it is perfectly acceptable to supplement one of the "real" cranberry sauces listed below with a single can of the jellied stuff, so long as you slice it into coins and don't spoon it out into a bowl as if it were dog food.

To make your own, all you need do is combine the tart berries with sugar in some kind of liquid, and allow the mixture to heat to the point where the berries burst. Stir the result and allow it to set into a kind of primitive jelly. Works every time, at least if you don't use too much liquid, and if you give the sauce time to set. All else that you might add—orange zest or sliced candied ginger, dried fruit, nuts, a splash of gin—is simply gild on a lily. (And delicious for that.)

——— BASIC CRANBERRY SAUCE ———

Cranberry sauce should be sweet but not cloying, and tart without causing pucker and anguish. It should have a jelly-like quality, but should owe more to the appearance of jam.

The key element to making cranberry sauce is to understand that cranberries are high in pectin, a carbohydrate that exists in many fruits and which is released by the berries when they are heated and the cells of the fruit break down. In the presence of sugar, which we add to cranberry sauce to offset its tanginess and acid, which is why the berries are tangy in the first place, the pectin molecules bond to one another, forming a kind of gel. The longer you cook a cranberry sauce, the more pectin is released and liquid is evaporated, and the stiffer the result will be.

Science! Sometimes it's helpful. So is spice. Some like a clove or two added to their cranberry sauce. (I am not one of them.) Others, a whisper of ginger and a small handful of nuts, for texture. Of this, I approve.

1 12-ounce bag fresh or thawed frozen cranberries
¾ cup sugar
¾ cup orange juice, preferably freshly squeezed
Zest of 1 orange, or to taste

1. Place cranberries in a small saucepan over medium-high heat and pour over these the sugar and orange juice. Stir to combine.

2. Cook until sugar is entirely melted and cranberries begin to burst in the heat, 4 to 6 minutes. Stir again, add zest, and cook for 2 or 3 minutes longer, turn off heat, cover pan, and allow to cool.

3. Put cranberry mixture in a serving bowl, cover, and place in refrigerator until cold, at least 2 hours, or until you need it.

——— GINGERED CRANBERRY SAUCE ———

½ cup pecans
1 12-ounce bag fresh or thawed frozen cranberries
¾ cup sugar
¾ cup orange juice, preferably freshly squeezed
1 teaspoon grated fresh ginger
Zest of 1 orange, or to taste

1. To toast pecans, spread nuts across the surface of a sauté pan set over medium heat. Allow to cook, tossing pecans occasionally until they turn fragrant, but do not burn. Immediately remove nuts from heat and set aside.

2. Place cranberries in a small saucepan over medium-high heat and pour over these the sugar and orange juice. Stir to combine.

3. Cook until sugar is entirely melted and cranberries begin to burst in the heat, 4 to 6 minutes. Stir again, add ginger and orange zest, and cook for 2 or 3 minutes longer, then turn off heat, add pecans, cover pan, and allow to cool.

4. Put cranberry mixture into a serving bowl, cover, and place in refrigerator until cold, at least 2 hours, or until you need it.

CHAPTER FIVE

SETTING THE TABLE, SERVING THE FOOD & SOME QUESTIONS OF ETIQUETTE

HERE ARE TWO THANKSGIVING truths. The first: a correctly set Thanksgiving table is of paramount importance to the success of your meal. It is the set on which the drama of the holiday plays out, and deserves to be as beautiful and considered as the food you have prepared for it.

I was cooking Thanksgiving once for a cast of outsiders, 20 of us jammed into a small Long Island cottage under cold, gray skies. There was a fire going in the front room and a table made of plywood next to it. The whole place smelled of turkey roasting, and wood smoke. A friend was opening oysters in the yard as fast and reliably as a metronome, and people stood around him drinking wine, beer, and whiskey. My wife unfolded a heavy linen tablecloth over the plywood, white as cream and ironed to a satin finish, and then put a long crimson runner over that. She added candles and some low-cut flowers in jam jars, then assembled our mismatched silverware and a stack of ironed cloth napkins. She laid out settings, added wine and water glasses, some cellars of salt and pepper.

It was a small house. The table filled most of it, and looked as resplendent as a silk-covered elephant sitting on a little stool. One of our friends came in from the yard and stopped still, shocked at the transformation.

"This is civilized," he said. "This is the whole thing, right here."

That is correct. Thanksgiving is a holiday that calls for a table set as if for a sacrament. No plastic should appear on your Thanksgiving table, no jugs of juice or soda or milk. There should be a neat cloth napkin for each person, and at the very least a knife and fork, a glass or two for water and wine, and a plate. There should be candles and flowers if you can manage and, if possible, all the food should be served on warmed platters, family style.

The second truth of Thanksgiving: very few people know how to do any of this. We understand the principle of place setting—everyone needs a plate and silverware, a glass for drinking, something on which to wipe one's mouth or fingers—but many are flummoxed by the particulars of how to arrange these things on a table correctly.

So we seek refuge in the comforts of fast-casual steam-table eating, with piles of plates and forks and knives and paper napkins set up in the kitchen, and a serve-yourself spread of Thanksgiving treats alongside it. Or, staring at a dining room table in fear, we panic and fall into the death spiral of improvisation. This is what leads people to stuff napkins into wine glasses, as if to make a flower. A napkin stuffed into a wine glass is tragic. It has no place at any table, not least a Thanksgiving one.

But setting a Thanksgiving table is simple.

Ideally, there should be a tablecloth, as thick as you can manage, clean and ironed. White is the classic color, but really anything that is not a pastel will do. Romantically, there might be that runner down the center, red and inviting, in honor of my wife. Absolutely there ought to be napkins, neatly folded in whatever manner you like so long as it does not resemble a bird.

You can have centerpieces, if you like—chrysanthemums, for instance, or lilies, some attractive fall foliage, a baby pumpkin or tiny gourd—but these must be low enough to allow everyone at the table to see everyone else across the expanse, and not be so large that you cannot set out food or condiments, candles or bottles of wine. A smart move: set the table with flowers, then remove them to sideboards or elsewhere just before you call everyone to the table.

There should be candles as well, as many as you can manage without overcrowding the table, or creating a fire hazard. (No scented candles. There are no exceptions to this rule.) Light these just before serving the food itself—no one wants candles guttering out during the meal itself. If you have candlesticks, polish them. If you don't, use votives instead. Place these in small glasses as at a little French bistro, or along a small piece of driftwood as if in a shelter magazine or romantic comedy.

Once you have the table covered with cloth, follow these simple steps to set each place.

1. Set out a dinner plate for each person, leaving enough room between plates for elbows and polite conversation. You can crowd people in, but the effect you are looking for should not suggest a mess hall.

2. Place a napkin to the left of each plate, with the folded spine aiming right.

3. Begin to lay out the silverware. Start with the knife, which should go to the immediate right of the plate, with the blade facing inward rather than outward. (A blade facing outward was once a sign of aggression. Now it's just the wrong way to set a knife on a table.) Follow with a soup spoon, if you're using one.

4. Place the entrée fork to the left of the plate, on top of the folded napkin or on the outside of a rolled one. (The etiquette police will tell you that the fork should never go on top of the napkin. The etiquette police have much bigger dining rooms and dining room tables than most of the rest of us.) If you were serving salad, you would place a salad fork to its left. (But you are not serving salad, because there is no place for salad at the Thanksgiving table.)

5. Place a dessert spoon and fork above the plate, if you're using these, with the spoon on top, its bowl to the left, and the fork below, its tines facing right. These should be smaller, slightly, than your entrée fork—there is no shame in substituting a salad fork or teaspoon for these.

6. Place a glass for water directly above the tip of the knife, and a wine glass to its right. If you plan on having more than one wine, and have enough wine glasses to support that habit, place these as follows, moving left to right: red wine glass, white wine glass, Champagne flute.

Looks good, no? But you are not done yet.

There should be kosher salt and either freshly ground black pepper or a pepper mill on the table as well, to accommodate those who like to season their own food; and hot sauce if you

1 Dinner plate

2 Napkin, with folded spine facing right

3 Knife, with blade facing in

4 Soup spoon (if using)

5 Entrée fork, placed on top of a folded napkin or on the outside of a rolled napkin

6 Dessert utensils, with bowl of spoon to the left and fork tines to the right

7 Water glass, placed directly above the tip of the knife

8 Wine glass (if using more than one, place in the following order: red wine glass, white wine glass, Champagne flute)

9 Place card

10 Centerpiece

11 Candles

are from the South, or peppered vinegar, or jalapeño jelly. These should be served, to the extent that this is possible, in noncommercial vessels. Salt cellars, pepper mills, and repurposed kitchenware beat labeled jars every time. Or almost every time: hot sauce, if it is part of your culture, may be served in the bottle in which it was sold.*

Now look at the set table again: Is there enough room left for platters of food? Try a dry run. Rustle up the platters you will be using and place these on the table bare, add empty gravy boats, a few wine bottles, whatever you think may take up the space. If it fits, it fits: you have a large table and ought to be proud of it. But if it doesn't, pull all the serving plates and add more candles and wine to the table to fill it up a little, and set up a food station somewhere near to the table that will allow your guests to serve themselves from the loaded-up platters without too much of a fuss. (You can, and should, leave the gravy and cranberry sauce on the table—these are, in the end, condiments that should be added at will, throughout the meal.) For a food station, lay out the platters in order—sliced turkey, starches and dressings, side dishes—and put a large serving spoon or fork on each.

---

* Who knows where this exception comes from, by the way, but it exists. Even my mother, who used to remove delivered pizza from its box when I was a child and serve it on a wide wooden platter, allows bottled hot sauce on her dinner table. Sometimes. And I once knew a mannered, gracious, and deeply imposing old Southern woman of the sort who makes a fine argument for the existence of a landed aristocracy in America indistinguishable from British royalty, who carried a small bottle of Tabasco sauce in her purse at all times.

HOW TO WARM PLATES AND PLATTERS

YOU HAVE MADE HOT food. You ought to serve it on warm china, rather than cold. This seems more a sensible act than a matter of etiquette (your food will stay warm longer), but it also depends on the room temperature of your home and on the climate in which you live. I grew up in the Northeast, in the sort of house where if things got chilly, my father would suggest putting on another sweater. I know from warming plates. If your family keeps the thermostat pinned to 80 or lives in Delray Beach, you will be fine with whatever is on the sideboard, as is. Just move along now. If not, here are three good ways to warm platters and plates.

1. Some dishwashers have a "plate warmer" function on them that you may never have used. It does exactly what it says it does.

2. If your dishwasher does not have that function, or if you don't have a dishwasher, use the oven. When you have finished cooking the turkey, and it is resting in advance of carving, turn the oven switch to "off." Then you can place your serving platters and plates into the empty space and allow them to absorb the leftover heat. Be careful. This method works astonishingly well.

3. You can do something similar on top of the stove if you're using the oven to heat food: just place the plates and platters on the stovetop, between burners or in range of the heat exhaust from the running oven, and rotate them every 10 minutes or so to spread the heat around.

Now it is time to eat. But who is sitting where? This is a question worth pondering well before people start to make their ways toward the table. Social engineering is as much a part of setting the Thanksgiving table as ironing napkins or polishing silver. You want to create a nice mix of ages and genders and worldviews, while at the same time avoiding the potential for political argument or personality clash. The Thanksgiving table is not the place to heal the rift between your sour Marxist aunt and her second cousin the Republican golf pro.

Sketch out some options on a sheet of paper: male, female, young, old. Separate spouses and children. Encourage delight. And then enlist children to make place cards that can sit to the top of each setting, above the dessert spoon and fork. Or, as Martha Stewart recommends, punch a hole in the corner of whatever they create, and use twine to tie it to a rolled napkin. (Another Martha Stewart tip: use neutral-colored card stock, or cream.)

Finally, as everyone takes a seat and prepares to eat, there is the delicate moment where you or someone at the table should ask for everyone's attention, and offer thanks to one and all for being present, and for helping out. This is extraordinarily important. Such literal thanks-giving may smack of religiosity to some, but it need not be spiritual in the least. It is the point of the entire exercise.

William Jennings Bryan wrote, "On Thanksgiving Day, we acknowledge our dependence." I think that's just about right. Give thanks.

CHAPTER SIX

DRINKS & DRINKING

I STARTED COOKING THANKSGIVING dinners in the late Reagan years, during the first flush of the wine merchant Georges Duboeuf's marketing campaign for Beaujolais nouveau. The wine was all over liquor stores and wine shops then, the cases covered with bright floral designs. Its low price and simple fruitiness seemed a perfect match for the holiday. We stored the stuff on the porch, and swilled it throughout the day: we thought it chilled sophistication, as we cooked.

Later, tastes shifted. My wife and I drank bubbly Prosecco before the meal, with oysters, and huge California Zinfandels and Meritages with the turkey, with bourbon to follow. (Once at a huge Thanksgiving out on Long Island, we drank sparkling wine throughout, from a huge silver tureen we called the loving cup, passing it endlessly around the table until the wine was gone, a three-hour toast.) There were years devoted to ancient, thin, fantastic old French vintages. Others to American Pinot Noirs, Italian Barbarescos. And always plenty of brown liquor to end the meal: Armagnac that my father insisted upon to create "the French hole" that allowed room for a second slice of pie; applejack for the virtuous pro-America crowd, or that bourbon again, or rye.

Always the meals were a success. There is no "right" wine for Thanksgiving, in other words, no must-have grape or vintage, cocktail, or spirit. Nor is there a "wrong" one, though I'd stay away from the low-end fortified stuff unless you are dining in a boxcar hurtling west. What you want is a variety of grapes and vintages. Encourage guests to bring wines that interest them, wines that they would like others to try. Additionally, you can lay in specialty items: beer for your uncle who only drinks Bud; nonalcoholic sparkling cider for the children; plenty of Diet Cokes and ashtrays for those who no longer drink.

Start serving the minute guests start to arrive, no matter the hour, and keep your own counsel about what each person chooses to drink and when. Thanksgiving is not a time to judge. For myself, I don't generally touch alcohol until dinner is served, but I know people who sip wine from morning onward to no ill effect, and even a few who commence the holiday with a tall, fragrant Manhattan. This seems excessive to me, a too-fast start to the festivities. But it is always 5 p.m. somewhere.

One of my brothers demands eggnog on Thanksgiving—the holiday marks the beginning of the Christmas season, is his view. (Really, he just loves eggnog.) My daughters demand hot apple cider. Some of my friends ask for mulled wine or hot buttered rum.

But there are really only a few hard-and-fast rules: There should be at least two bottles of cold fizzy water available per adult present at a Thanksgiving meal—an aid to digestion and an enemy of dehydration alike. And whatever wines you have, you should have quite a bit of. You should be stocked so that running out of the stuff during a Thanksgiving meal would be a shock. A bottle of wine per person present is not at all too much.

TOBY'S EGGNOG

In the matter of egg-based cocktails, my brother does not fool around. A single glass of this '50s-style eggnog should suffice to fell a large person. The correct dosage is a small teacupful. It would pair excellently with a Chesterfield cigarette and news from Korea.

10 eggs, separated
¾ cup sugar
4 cups heavy cream
4 cups whole milk
2 cups brandy
1 cup rye whiskey
1 cup dark rum
½ cup sherry
½ teaspoon kosher salt
Grated nutmeg, to taste

1. In an electric mixer, beat egg yolks with sugar until thick. Slowly add cream and milk and beat until thick. Slowly add liquors while continuing to beat at slow speed. Chill in refrigerator for several hours.

2. Add salt to egg whites. Beat until nearly stiff. Fold whipped egg whites into the yolk mixture. Chill in refrigerator for at least 2 hours.

3. Pour eggnog into punch cups or a glass, and sprinkle top with freshly grated nutmeg.

——————— HOT APPLE CIDER ———————

A fall and winter staple in our home, where it has all but replaced hot chocolate for its warming qualities and spiced excellence. Do not allow the mixture to boil, but make sure to simmer it for at least 15 minutes for maximum flavor.

2 quarts apple cider
¼ cup light brown sugar
2 cinnamon sticks
6 allspice berries
6 green cardamom pods
1 large orange, cut into quarters
⅓ teaspoon kosher salt
Grated nutmeg

1. In a large pot set over medium heat, warm the cider. Add the brown sugar and stir until it dissolves, then add cinnamon, allspice, cardamom, orange, and salt.

2. Bring mixture to a slight simmer and allow to steep for at least 30 minutes. Do not allow to boil. Grate nutmeg over the top to taste.

THE ROLE OF OYSTERS AT THANKSGIVING

YOU HAVE PERHAPS NOTED that I do not support the idea of serving appetizers at Thanksgiving? They get in the way of the meal both by taking up valuable stomach space and by wasting dishes and the time spent cleaning them.

Oysters are a different matter entirely. Laying in a few dozen bivalves to eat while the turkey rests on a sidebar is in my view a brilliant solution to the fidgety issue of serving food in advance of the Thanksgiving meal. Consumed with a sparkling wine, outdoors if possible, oysters provide a direct and visceral connection to aquatic harvest, and to the true history of Thanksgiving in America.

Opening them is difficult, of course, at least until you get the hang of it. Practice has its own rewards.

All you need is a table, a cutting board, a dish towel or two, and an oyster knife. Each oyster has a top and a bottom. The "cup" side is the bottom one. Place the oyster cup side down on a dish towel. Using another dish towel to protect your left hand (if you are right-handed), grip the oyster carefully with its narrow, triangular hinge facing you. Insert the tip of the oyster knife into the top of that hinge and turn the knife tip to the right, as if using a key to open a lock. The combination of gentle force and torque should break the hinge and allow you to insert the knife into the oyster.

Slide the knife around the outside of the shell, loosening it from the bottom cup. (Try not to lose too much of

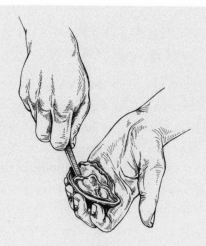

the liquor in there!) Use the knife to scrape the oyster
from the top shell and allow it to drop into the bottom
cup. Discard top shell.

Now separate the meat from the bottom shell. Scrape
the knife along the inside of the shell under the meat.
Once it has separated, the oyster is ready. Use the tip of
the knife to remove any spare bits of shell, and serve with
copious amounts of sparkling wine. Grated horseradish,
cocktail sauce, sliced lemons, and hot sauce are acceptable
accompaniments. Mignonettes are not, not today.

———— MULLED WINE ————

I will forever associate mulled wine with a winter night I spent once at the Bread & Puppet compound in Glover, Vermont, singing madrigals. I was 13 and had made my way there with older friends, to attend the funeral of an avant-garde theater director who worked at our Brooklyn school. One of his last productions: *The Resistible Rise of Arturo Ui*, by Bertolt Brecht. It was a different time.

We flew bird puppets around in a big field and then crowded into a barn in the dark. There was a hurdy-gurdy, and all these women with big church voices out of the past, and men smoking in the doorway, their faces lighted by the fireplace or cigarettes or both, and enough wine to float our memories into the inky black sky. I couldn't say it then, because I was 13 and a boy from the city with a skateboard and anger issues. But it was so, so great.

This drink tastes of that night, and is perfect for one of those Thanksgiving weekends where the air smells of snow. If you want to get fancy, wrap the cinnamon, cardamom, peppercorns, and cloves in a sheet of cheesecloth and tie it off with string, so that people don't end up with bits of spice in their glass. But this is not necessary.

2½ cups sugar
3 cups water
4 cinnamon sticks, approximately 3 inches each
10 green cardamom pods
6 black peppercorns

8 whole cloves
2 bottles of dry red wine
2 vanilla beans, halved lengthwise
1 orange, cut into quarters

1. In a large pot set over high heat, bring the sugar and water to a boil, stirring until the sugar dissolves.

2. Add the cinnamon sticks, cardamom pods, peppercorns, and cloves, then the wine, and then the vanilla beans and the orange. Reduce heat to low and simmer, uncovered, for at least 10 minutes. Do not allow to boil.

HOT BUTTERED RUM

Eggnog is a dessert in alcoholic form. Mulled wine is tea made into an adult beverage. Hot buttered rum is just a soul warmer, exactly the right drink to have in the wake of a brisk post-Thanksgiving walk in the chill, perhaps accompanied by cigars or leaf burning. It combines tastes of colonial-era trade (rum, brown sugar, Caribbean spices) with British-style scalding water, to marvelous effect. This recipe is for two good-sized mugs. Double or triple as needed.

2 tablespoons unsalted butter
2 scant tablespoons light brown sugar
2 pinches ground cinnamon
2 pinches grated nutmeg
2 whole cloves
2 allspice berries
4 ounces golden or dark rum

1. Place 1 tablespoon each of butter in the bottom of two mugs, and a tablespoon each of the brown sugar. Using the back of a spoon, cream these together, adding a pinch of the cinnamon and nutmeg to each mug.

2. Place a clove and an allspice berry in each mug, and 2 ounces of rum.

3. Top with boiling water and serve immediately. Whipped cream, if you have some, would not be a terrible addition to the top of the drink.

CHAPTER SEVEN

DESSERT

THE ROLE OF DESSERT in a properly prepared Thanksgiving feast most closely resembles the final step in a tactical shooting drill used by the military in close-combat situations. Some call it the Mozambique drill. Two shots from a handgun are placed in the target's center mass, followed by a carefully aimed third to the head. In terms of entertaining, the Mozambique drill means the turkey and sides can do significant damage. But the kill shot is pie.

That's what my mother taught me, anyway. A proper Thanksgiving should close out with a blast of warm, gooey flavor—a burst of sugar that can give a guest just enough energy to make it from table to couch, the holiday's final resting place.

The dessert need not be extravagant. It absolutely should not be experimental. Nor should it be overly cute. Dessert at Thanksgiving must not involve individual tartlets or parfaits, nor marshmallows in any form. Frosted cakes are unnecessary. Save the chocolate for nights of depression and anxiety—for New Year's Eve, or an unwelcome birthday. Instead, focus on the proper execution of the American classics: apple pie, for instance, with a mound of whipped cream, or pumpkin pie with same. These represent Thanksgiving's highest achievement. They are an explanation of American exceptionalism, made in pastry form. The right apple pie is a trump to beat all comers.

In some families, it is traditional to farm out the baking of Thanksgiving pies and making of desserts to guests. (If you find yourself as a guest at someone else's Thanksgiving, there is no finer gift to bring than a pie and a bottle of brown liquor.) With time and oven space at a premium in the hours leading up to the feast, this practice can make a great deal of sense. And the sight of friends and relatives arriving on your doorstep on Thanksgiving bearing pumpkin pies or apple cobblers, berry crisps or Indian puddings, can warm the heart.

But dangers lurk. Aunts can go rogue. Jell-O may make an appearance, or peanut butter, or sorbet. It is best to be prepared for this eventuality. Take out insurance. On the weekend before Thanksgiving, you should always, always, make a pie yourself.

———————————— APPLE PIE ————————————

You can make an apple pie with bacon fat in the dough, or with a lattice of Cheddar cheese across the top, the interior studded with raisins. But not on Thanksgiving. What is preferable here, at least until you have made it for a few years and grown bored of the excellence, is the plain-Jane original.

And this is it. Scented with autumnal spice and caramelizing sugars, it is apple pie to call to mind the Homer Price stories of Robert McCloskey. It tastes of baseball divinity. Pair it with vanilla ice cream or whipped cream, along with a glass of applejack or milk, depending on your age, recreational history, and taste.

2 recipes all-purpose pie dough, well chilled
    (page 99)
2 tablespoons unsalted butter
2½ pounds apples (5 large Honeycrisps will do it),
    peeled and cored, then cut into wedges
¼ teaspoon ground allspice
½ teaspoon ground cinnamon
¼ teaspoon kosher salt
⅔ cup plus 1 tablespoon sugar
2 tablespoons all-purpose flour
2 teaspoons cornstarch
1 tablespoon cider vinegar
1 large egg, lightly beaten

1. Place a large baking sheet on the middle rack of the oven and preheat to 425 degrees. Remove one disc of dough from the refrigerator and, using a pin, roll it out on a lightly floured surface until it is roughly 12 inches in diameter. Fit this crust into a 9-inch pie plate, trimming it to leave a ½-inch overhang. (Make sure to use a light hand with the flour you sprinkle on your work surface when you are rolling out the crust. It can toughen the dough. Well-chilled pastry dough does not need much in the way of extra flour to keep it from sticking.) Place this plate, with the dough, in the freezer.

2. In a large sauté pan set over medium-high heat, melt the

butter and add apples to the pan. Stir to coat fruit with butter and cook, stirring occasionally. Meanwhile, whisk together the spices, salt, and ⅔ cup sugar, and sprinkle this over the pan, stirring to combine. Lower the heat and cook until apples have started to soften, approximately 5 to 7 minutes. Sprinkle the flour and cornstarch over the apples and continue to cook, stirring occasionally, another 3 to 5 minutes. Remove pan from heat, add cider vinegar, stir, scrape fruit mixture into a bowl, and allow to cool completely. (The fruit mixture will cool faster if spread out on a rimmed baking sheet.)

3. Roll out the remaining dough disc on a lightly floured surface until it is roughly 10 or 11 inches in diameter.

4. Remove pie crust from freezer and put the cooled pie filling into it. Cover with remaining dough. Press the edges together, trim the excess, then crimp the edges with the tines of a fork. Using a sharp knife, cut three or four steam vents in the top of the crust. Lightly brush the top of the pie with beaten egg and sprinkle with remaining tablespoon of sugar.

5. Place pie on hot baking sheet in oven and bake for 20 minutes, then reduce temperature to 375 degrees. Continue to cook until the interior is bubbling and the crust is golden brown, roughly 30 to 40 minutes more. Remove and allow to cool, about 2 hours.

ALL-PURPOSE PIE DOUGH

PASTRY DOUGH IS JUST flour and fat, brought together with water. I add a splash of acidity and a bit of salt for flavor. This recipe makes enough dough to create a single pie crust. Double it for a pie with a top crust. Most recipes warn not to overwork the dough, because this can make the pastry tough. If you use enough fat, though, this is rarely a problem. A pastry chef at a New York restaurant told me this once, sternly: "Don't be afraid to push it around a little, enough to get the butter in there and for the dough to come together." She was right. The last thing you want when you are rolling out your dough is for it all to fall apart.

Additional tips: When making pie-dough recipes, do not ignore adjectives relating to temperature. "Cold butter" means butter taken directly from the refrigerator. "Ice water" means water in a glass that has a lot of ice in it.

Some cooks require the blind baking of pie shells before a filling is added—this means that they are cooked ahead of time in a 425 degree oven beneath a blanket of parchment paper or foil weighted down with old dried beans or pie weights, or a few handfuls of coins. It adds an extra 20 minutes or so to the process and can mean the difference between a doughy pie bottom and a shatteringly crisp one. On this front, I am agnostic. You do not have to blind-bake a Thanksgiving pie shell in order to cook pie correctly.

But you do need to make the dough. There is a place in American cooking for store-bought frozen pie shells. You can use them for brunch quiches in the style of the 1970s, or for bake-sale pies. But for Thanksgiving you must make your own crust, always. The difference is notable in both flavor and texture, and is important to the success of the holiday as a whole. Pre-made pie shells represent a corner not worth cutting.

Finally, you should not make pie dough in a kitchen in which you are also roasting a turkey and simmering stock and boiling potatoes for mash. You want a chilly environment, not a tropical one, so that the dough stays cool as you make it. The kitchen temperature you want for dough is that of a fall morning in New England, the sort where you get out of bed and pad around the house in pajamas, wool socks, and a sweater, and the kids ask if you can turn up the heat.

1¼ cups all-purpose flour
3 tablespoons unsalted butter, cold, cut into ½-inch cubes
1 tablespoon vegetable shortening, cold
1 pinch kosher salt
Yolk of 1 egg, beaten
½ teaspoon cider vinegar
½ cup ice water

1. Using your fingertips or the pulse function of a food processor, blend together the flour, fats, and salt until the mixture resembles a coarse meal. There should be pebbles of butter throughout the mixture.

2. Add egg yolk and vinegar to ½ cup ice water and stir to combine. Drizzle 2 tablespoons of this mixture over the dough and gently stir or pulse to combine. Gather a golf-ball-sized bit of dough and squeeze to combine. If it does not hold together, add a little more of the liquid and stir or pulse, then check again. Repeat as necessary.

3. Turn the dough out onto a lightly floured surface and gather together into a rough ball. You want to be careful not to overwork the flour, but not too careful; the dough should hold together. Divide the ball in half with a knife or a pastry scraper, then divide each portion in half again, to create four portions. Using the heel of your hand, flatten each portion of dough once or twice to expand the pebbles of butter, then gather the dough together again in one ball.

4. Flatten the ball into a 5- or 6-inch disc and dust lightly with flour. Wrap the disc in plastic wrap and place in the refrigerator for at least 60 minutes.

PECAN PIE

It is hard to say when exactly the food cognoscenti turned against corn syrup, a silken suspension of glucose-rich corn sugar that plays a significant part in many recipes for pecan pie.

It may be that corn syrup suffers in the shadow of its corporate cousin, high-fructose corn syrup. High-fructose corn syrup is created by treating corn syrup with enzymes in order to pro-duce fructose—a sweeter sugar than glucose. High-fructose corn syrup can be found in seemingly every third packaged product on your supermarket shelves, from bread to commercial bratwurst. There may or may not be a link between the rise in its use and the explosion of obesity among our nation's populace. The science is mixed. But when high-fructose corn syrup is mixed with plain corn syrup, as it often is under the guise of the "Light Corn Syrup" sold on supermarket shelves, the result imparts a toothachingly bright flavor, and a faint plastic texture, to pies.

So update your eyeglass prescription. Read the fine print before you buy.

Or go elsewhere in the pantry to find a sweetener that will not crystallize in the high heat of the oven, as plain sugar does, making it a poor candidate for pie. A light corn syrup that contains no high-fructose corn syrup makes an exceedingly good, moist pecan pie. But I have matched or exceeded its pleasures with maple syrup, with sorghum, and notably with golden syrup, a honey-hued concoction of British extraction that may be too colonial in flavor for our use on such a proudly American holiday. (Still, if you can find it? As Julia Child taught us, you are alone in the kitchen. No one need know.)

What follows is a recipe that allows the use of any of these sweeteners in conjunction with light brown sugar. Scented by vanilla, bourbon, and the strong nuttiness of toasted pecans, the result is a pie that is as much candy as pastry. It is not for the faint of heart. Its deliciousness is gigantic.

1 recipe all-purpose pie dough, well chilled
   (page 99)
2 cups pecans

5 tablespoons unsalted butter
1 cup packed light brown sugar
¾ cup light corn syrup, maple syrup, sorghum, or
    golden syrup
1 teaspoon kosher salt
2 tablespoons bourbon
2 teaspoons vanilla extract
3 large eggs, beaten

1. For the crust, use a rolling pin to roll the well-chilled disc of dough out on a lightly floured surface until it is roughly 12 inches in diameter. Fit this crust into a 9-inch pie plate, trimming it to leave a ½-inch overhang. (Make sure to use a light hand with the flour you sprinkle on your work surface when you are rolling out the crust. It can toughen the dough. Well-chilled pastry dough does not need much in the way of extra flour to keep it from sticking.) Place this plate, with the dough, in the freezer and chill for roughly 15 or 20 minutes.

2. Preheat oven to 350 degrees. Spread the pecans out on a rimmed baking sheet and bake in oven, shaking the pan often, until the nuts are fragrant, approximately 7 to 10 minutes. Remove from oven and allow to cool. Roughly chop about half the nuts.

3. Make the filling. In a saucepan set over medium heat, combine the butter, brown sugar, syrup, and salt. Bring this mixture to a boil, stirring constantly, and continue to boil for a minute or so. Remove from the heat and stir in the nuts, bourbon, and vanilla, then set aside to cool slightly, about 5 minutes. Whisk the eggs into the filling until smooth.

4. Remove the pie crust from the freezer. Prick the bottom of the shell all over with the tines of a fork. (Unnecessary if you

have blind-baked the shell.) Place the pie plate on a baking sheet and pour the filling into it. Bake pie on the middle rack of oven for 45 minutes to 1 hour, checking after 20 minutes or so to see if the crust is browning too quickly. (If it is, loosely place a crown of aluminum foil around the edges.) Remove from the oven when the filling has set and gone a little puffy—it should jiggle only slightly. Allow to cool on a rack. Serve warm or at room temperature, with plain whipped cream.

WHIPPED CREAM

WHIPPED CREAM GOES WELL with nearly every Thanksgiving dessert. You can easily omit the sugar and vanilla if you prefer a savory note atop your sweets.

1 cup heavy cream
¼ cup sugar
1 teaspoon vanilla extract

1. In a large mixing bowl, whip cream until it just begins to form stiff peaks.
2. Add sugar and vanilla, and whip again until the cream holds its peaks.

PUMPKIN PIE

Squash was central to those first Thanksgivings with the Wampanoag, and pumpkin pie in one form or another has been a part of Thanksgiving since at least the late eighteenth century. The grim business of the Atlantic triangle trade brought Caribbean spices and molasses into the shell, and British whipped cream for the top.

Traditionally made in modern America with canned pumpkin purée (really, a mixture of fall squashes, including pumpkin) and, often, evaporated milk, pumpkin pie is an assemblage as much as it is a recipe. It rewards devotion to a 1950s ideal of mechanized food preparation, what the television personality Sandra Lee would later call cooking that is "semi homemade."

So you can shop for a pie pumpkin (much smaller than the Halloween model, sometimes called a sugar pumpkin), cut it in half, scoop out the seeds, and bake until soft, then scoop out the softened flesh to make a purée. This takes a very long time. You can add to this egg yolks, sugar, and sour cream. You might add maple syrup. Or cream cheese. But these tweaks and improvements are difficult work and will not please those for whom memory is made of a pie created from canned pumpkin and evaporated milk. So in the spirit of inclusion, let us celebrate this reminder of our twentieth-century past.

1 recipe all-purpose pie dough, well chilled
    (page 99)
2 tablespoons granulated sugar
2 tablespoons light brown sugar

2 tablespoons molasses
½ teaspoon kosher salt
1½ teaspoons ground cinnamon
½ teaspoon ground ginger
¼ teaspoon ground cloves
2 large eggs
1 15-ounce can pumpkin purée
1½ cups evaporated milk (or whole milk, or light
   cream)

1. For the crust, use a rolling pin to roll the well-chilled disc of dough out on a lightly floured surface until it is roughly 12 inches in diameter. Fit this crust into a 9-inch pie plate, trimming it to leave a ½-inch overhang. (Make sure to use a light hand with the flour you sprinkle on your work surface when you are rolling out the crust. It can toughen the dough. Well-chilled pastry dough does not need much in the way of extra flour to keep it from sticking.) Place this plate, with the dough, in the freezer and chill for roughly 15 or 20 minutes.

2. Preheat oven to 425 degrees. Combine the sugars, molasses, salt, and spices in a small bowl. Beat the eggs in a large mixing bowl and add the pumpkin purée and the sugar-and-spice mixture. Gradually add the evaporated milk and beat to combine.

3. Remove the chilled pie shell from the freezer and pour the pumpkin mixture into it. Place the pie on the center rack in the oven and cook for 15 minutes, then rotate pie and reduce heat to 350 degrees. Cook for an additional 45 to 50 minutes, or until a knife or toothpick inserted in the center of the pie comes out clean. Remove and allow to cool, about 2 hours. Serve with whipped cream, if desired. (Pie can also be refrigerated and served cold.)

—————— APPLE PIZZA ——————

There is no surer way to improve upon a classic dish than to cook it with children. My kids came up with this variation on an old *Gourmet* magazine recipe for apple galette by making it weekly with their friend Linell Hanover, streamlining the process along the way. Their efforts transformed the result from classic French country cooking to modern American melting-pot excellence. My wife added a flash of bourbon and a few tablespoons of fig preserves. The kids recoiled in horror. Until they tasted the result.

1 recipe pizza pastry dough (page 109)
2½ pounds apples (5 or 6 large Honeycrisps will do it),
    peeled, cored, and cut into slices
1 tablespoon lemon juice
⅔ cup plus 2 teaspoons sugar
½ cup water
2 tablespoons fig preserves
½ teaspoon lemon zest
1 pinch ground cinnamon
4 tablespoons bourbon
3 tablespoons unsalted butter, cut into small cubes

1. Line a baking sheet with parchment paper or a Silpat sheet. Roll out the disc of pastry dough on a lightly floured surface until it resembles a bare, rustic pizza of about 15 inches in diameter. Carefully peel this off the counter and place it on the baking sheet, gently folding over the edges so that it fits on the sheet. Place in freezer for at least 30 minutes while preparing the filling.

2. Preheat oven to 425 degrees. In a large bowl, toss most of the apple slices with the lemon juice and ⅓ cup of the sugar, reserving a full handful of apple slices on the side. Place the sugared apples in a heavy saucepan set over high heat, and add the water, another ⅓ cup sugar, the fig preserves, lemon zest, and cinnamon. When it reaches a boil, reduce heat, cover, and cook at a low simmer for approximately 20 minutes. Remove lid and continue to cook until most of the liquid has evaporated, approximately another 5 minutes. Add bourbon and cook another 5 to 7 minutes, then remove from heat and mash apples roughly with a fork. Set aside and allow to cool.

3. Remove dough from freezer and unfold edges so pastry is flat. Spread the cooled apple-fig mixture all over the pastry, leaving a 2-inch border. Place remaining sliced apples on top of this, spreading them evenly over the apple-fig sauce. Fold bare edges of dough back over filling, partially covering the apples, to create a raised crust, slightly resembling that of a pizza. Dot apples with butter. Brush edges lightly with water, and dust with remaining 2 teaspoons sugar. Bake until pastry is golden and apples are very tender, approximately 45 minutes.

PIZZA PASTRY DOUGH

SWEETER THAN A REGULAR pie dough, this recipe works just as well with improvised fruit toppings—a mixture of pear and apple, say, or strawberry and rhubarb—as it does in our Thanksgiving apple version. It also yields enough dough for a double-crust pie. Simply divide the final portion in half, flatten each portion into a 5- or 6-inch disc,

and dust lightly with flour. Wrap the discs in plastic wrap
and place in the refrigerator for at least 60 minutes.

> *2½ cups all-purpose flour*
> *8 ounces unsalted butter, cold, cut into ½-inch pieces*
> *2 teaspoons sugar*
> *¾ teaspoon kosher salt*
> *½ cup plus a few tablespoons ice water*

1. Using your fingertips or the pulse function of a food
processor, blend together the flour, butter, sugar, and salt
until the mixture resembles a coarse meal. There should
be pebbles of butter throughout the mixture.

2. Drizzle the ½ cup ice water over this mixture and
gently stir or pulse to combine. Gather a golf-ball-sized
bit of dough and squeeze to combine. If it does not hold
together, add a tablespoon more of ice water and stir or
pulse, then check again. Repeat as necessary.

3. Turn the dough out onto a lightly floured surface
and gather together into a rough ball. You want to be careful not to overwork the flour, but not too careful; the
dough should hold together. Divide the ball in half with a
knife or a pastry scraper, then divide each portion in half
again, and again, to create eight portions. Using the heel
of your hand, flatten each portion of dough once or twice
to expand the pebbles of butter, then gather the dough
together again in one ball.

4. Flatten the ball into a 5- or 6-inch disc and dust
lightly with flour. Wrap the disc in plastic wrap and place
in the refrigerator for at least 60 minutes.

APPLE CRISP

Here is what amounts to a deconstructed apple pie, a messy concoction of fruit covered with a crumbled topping. (Some call the dish a "crumble." A cobbler has a biscuit topping.) Baked in a hot oven, it results in a dessert of remarkable flexibility—the sort of dish that can be put together on the fly, or improvised upon with almost universal success. In the summer you might substitute berries or peaches, or a combination thereof in place of the apples. But not on Thanksgiving. On Thanksgiving, only apples are appropriate.

2½ pounds apples (5 large Honeycrisps will do it),
    peeled and cored, then cut into wedges
1 tablespoon lemon juice
¾ cup sugar
¼ teaspoon ground cloves
½ teaspoon ground cinnamon
½ cup all-purpose flour, sifted
1 pinch kosher salt
6 tablespoons unsalted butter, cut into small pieces

1. Preheat oven to 350 degrees. Place the apple wedges into a large mixing bowl and add the lemon juice, ¼ cup of the sugar, and all the spices, and mix to combine. Pour this mixture into a buttered casserole dish.

2. Using your fingertips or the pulse function of a food processor, blend together the flour, remaining ½ cup sugar, the salt, and butter until the mixture resembles a coarse meal. There

should be pebbles of butter throughout the mixture. Sprinkle this over the apple mixture. Bake for 45 minutes to 1 hour, or until the apples are completely tender and the crust has gone golden brown in the heat.

PEAR COBBLER

Another dish that lends itself well to non-Thanksgiving preparations, this cobbler is terrific with raspberries or blackberries, depending on the season, and with mixtures of berries and apples, berries and pears, apples and pears. It takes its name from the cobblestone appearance of the dough on top of the fruit. The addition of a spray of diced candied ginger to the fruit before you lay down the pieces of dough will yield a fragrance and fiery excellence that is very close to fancy grade.

> *2½ pounds pears, peeled and cored, then cut into*
> *wedges (6–8 medium-sized pears will do it)*
> *½ cup plus 3 tablespoons sugar*
> *1 tablespoon lemon juice*
> *Zest of 1 lemon*
> *2 tablespoons diced candied ginger (optional)*
> *2 cups all-purpose flour*
> *1 tablespoon baking powder*
> *½ teaspoon kosher salt*
> *6 tablespoons unsalted butter, cold, cut into small*
> *pieces*
> *1 large egg*
> *½ cup whole milk*

1. Preheat oven to 425 degrees. Butter a 9-inch cast-iron skillet or 8-inch square baking dish. Place the fruit in a large bowl, and add ½ cup sugar and the lemon juice and zest. Gently mix until the sugar dissolves. Transfer to the skillet and top with candied ginger, if using.

2. Sift together the flour, baking powder, salt, and 1 tablespoon sugar. Add the butter and, using a fork, work it together with the dry ingredients until the mixture is coarse. In a separate bowl, stir the egg and milk until combined. Pour over the flour and butter mixture and stir to combine into a smooth dough.

3. Using your fingers, place clumps of dough the size of golf balls on top of the fruit mixture, pressing down slightly to create a rough-textured, cobbled crust. Sprinkle with remaining 2 tablespoons sugar and bake until the top is golden brown, about 30 to 45 minutes. Allow to cool slightly before serving.

INDIAN PUDDING

Here is a taste of old New England, of the Durgin Park restaurant in Boston, and of my grandmother's house on an island in Maine. The British would call it nursery food. It is mush, essentially, thick with the dark flavor of molasses. It is not at all pretty. But it is phenomenally delicious. When you swirl in some fresh cream at the end, it begins to exhibit a rough, homespun beauty that evokes this nation's beginnings.

4 cups whole milk
4 tablespoons unsalted butter

½ cup yellow cornmeal
½ cup molasses
3 large eggs, beaten
1 teaspoon ground cinnamon
½ teaspoon ground ginger
1 teaspoon kosher salt
1 cup yellow raisins

1. Preheat oven to 300 degrees. Heat the milk and butter together in a large saucepan until it just boils, then keep warm over low heat.

2. In a mixing bowl, combine the cornmeal and molasses. Slowly add approximately ½ cup of the scalded milk to the mixture, stirring constantly to combine. Add the eggs and stir again to combine. Carefully pour this mixture into the saucepan with the scalded milk and stir until smooth. Add the spices, salt, and raisins, and stir again.

3. Pour the mixture into a 2½-quart buttered baking dish, place dish in a pan of hot water, and put in oven. Bake for 60 to 90 minutes, or until firm but not dry. Allow to cool for 30 minutes or so. Serve with whipped cream, plain cream, or vanilla ice cream.

CHAPTER EIGHT

CLEANUP & LEFTOVERS

T HIS IS IT. EVERYONE is leaving now, packing up leftovers and memories, heading back home. It has been a marvelous holiday, celebrated well. And now it is time to clean up.

Really? Yes, really. Now. There are no exceptions to the clean-up-tonight rule. Leave the kitchen gleaming so that the morning may dawn a new day, not a continuation of this one. The last thing you want to do on the morning after Thanksgiving is to walk into a kitchen filled with piles of dirty dishes, a platoon of dead bottles, the sink filled with pots and pans. These are what medical professionals call depression triggers. Holidays are hard enough without courting changes in your limbic system.

Before even the first guest arrives, think about your holiday endgame: how to tackle all the dishes, cutlery, glasses, pots, and pans that will end up in your kitchen after their use. Have plenty of dish soap on hand for the washing, and two or three new sponges, some nonabrasive cleaner. Lay in paper towels, some dish rags, a spray bottle of surface cleaner—a complete Johnny Dishwasher night-porter package. Thanksgiving is an exhausting affair a daylong excursion into a world of service and hospitality that most of us visit only once or twice a year. But the rules of that world are absolute and important. Restaurant people clean as they go. They keep their work stations clean. You should aim to do the same.

Do not be afraid to delegate. If you are planning a break between the service of dinner and dessert, an hour in which your guests may take a walk through the brisk air of your neighborhood, detail a few people to stay behind to knock down the dinner plates and silverware, all that has been dirtied in the name of the savory course. The exercise is similar, as are the re-

wards. Then, after dessert, repeat the process, this time in ear-
nest. Ask someone to haul all the bottles out to the recycling
bin. Have someone else gather all the dirty linens into a pile.
Designate a plate brigade, a leftovers team, a pot washer, a glass
collector, a trash man, a saint of guttered candles and spilled
wax. The teamwork underscores the collaborative element of a
feast meant to celebrate the sharing of our bounty—both in
food and in refuse.

Additionally, lay in some to-go containers to send people
home with leftovers at meal's end: pint containers of dressing,
Brussels sprouts, mashed potatoes, slices of turkey. This will
leave some room in the refrigerator for the leftovers you yourself
will need in coming days. These can be assembled as others
scrub down around you, and left to sit as everyone decamps to

soft seats for a thorough debriefing of the evening and the slow slide into the end of the evening.

And when, precisely, is that? It is perhaps the most vexing question to surround a properly prepared Thanksgiving feast. When does the long day come, finally, to an end?

For a few years in my family we finished Thanksgivings with a movie, a dozen people crammed into a room designed to hold half that number, everyone sprawled in front of the glowing hearth of a television, some asleep, some soon to be that way. Thanksgivings came to a close with the rolling credits of Ron Howard's *The Paper* or the original *Godzilla*. Other times we simply sat, crushed by happy indulgence, until someone made the first move to go. Neither was an unhappy outcome.

Some, though, prefer finality. The American historian William Hogeland used to say, "It is time for you to go." Hogeland would proclaim this at the end of long evenings at his Brooklyn brownstone, reclined deep in a sofa in his living room, the sinks in the kitchen piled high with the detritus of a feast. It was hardly a judgment on the company. Many, many hours had been spent eating and drinking with friends and family, talking and laughing, arguing and laughing all the more. We might have thought ourselves pleased to linger into early morning, all of us crashed around the living room fighting the inevitable end of a glorious evening. There was always somewhere another bottle of wine, another splash of bourbon or glass of water. We could have gone the distance. But really it was time. Hogeland marked it loudly, in good cheer, and off we went, laughing, secure in the accuracy of his pronouncement, back to our own homes, happy as can be.

Whether you can be so bold or whether you simply retreat to the kitchen to finish the cleaning until your guests take the hint, is the choice of the host. But actual rudeness is to be avoided at all costs. As in all social engagements, people will figure things out eventually.

"That was a good party." This is all you want people to say. And tomorrow there will be leftovers.

—— A PROPER TURKEY SANDWICH ——

The best Thanksgiving turkey sandwich is the first one, assembled soon after a stirring of hunger finally returns to the belly of the person making it, barefoot, in a quiet kitchen lighted only by the dim bulb above the stove and the harsh glare of the one in the refrigerator. As with virtually all dishes made with leftovers, a leftover turkey sandwich can be as simple or as complicated as you like. What follows is merely a starting point. Racy diners might sprinkle some curry powder on the mayonnaise before closing the sandwich. Others might lay some leftover carrots across the meat, soft and sweet. And if any gravy remains, cold and congealed in a cup in the refrigerator? Spread a teaspoon or two of it across the bread in place of, or in addition to, the cranberry sauce. That qualifies as professional-grade turkey sandwich making.

2 slices thick-cut bread
1 tablespoon mayonnaise
1 tablespoon cranberry sauce
1 tablespoon leftover Thanksgiving dressing (pages 49–53)
1 scant handful of turkey meat (ideally, dark meat and skin)
1 piece romaine lettuce, washed, dried, and ripped in half

1. Toast bread so that it has a crisp exterior but remains soft within.

2. Spread mayonnaise thickly on one piece of bread, cranberry sauce on the other. Spread the stuffing on top of the cranberry sauce, and cover with meat, then the romaine. Top sandwich with the piece of toast spread with the mayonnaise.

——————— TURKEY À LA KING ———————

Turkey à la King is the General Tso's Chicken of Thanksgiving leftover meals, a dish rich in origin myth that is generally delicious even when prepared with spectacular ineptitude. It has nothing to do with royalty. It is either the invention of a Philadelphia hotel cook named King, who became famous for making the dish (with chicken) in the late nineteenth century, or the creation of some other hotel cook who made a similar dish (also with chicken) for a patron named King, who became famous for eating it. Or it is something else entirely. But blood-royal kings are not involved. This is America! Our kings are Kings.

You can add to the recipe a splash of cream or a cup of peas (or both). You can whisk an egg yolk into the sauce as if you were a French chef. You can use less roux. But do not ever go light on the butter.

6 tablespoons unsalted butter
4 tablespoons all-purpose flour
1 to 2 cups turkey stock (page 19)
1 cup sliced mushrooms, the wilder the better
1 red bell pepper, seeded and cut into thin strips
1½ cups chopped cooked turkey, in small pieces

2 tablespoons dry sherry
Kosher salt and freshly ground black pepper to taste
Finely chopped parsley, for garnish

1. Make a roux. In a small saucepan set over medium heat, melt 4 tablespoons of the butter until it starts to foam. Sprinkle the flour over the butter and stir to combine, then cook, stirring often, until it begins to take on the color of straw, approximately 5 to 10 minutes.

2. Slowly add 1 cup of turkey stock to this mixture, and stir to combine. Add more stock to thin the sauce to your liking. Keep warm.

3. In a large sauté pan set over medium-high heat, melt the remaining 2 tablespoons butter until it foams. Add the mushrooms and bell pepper and cook, stirring often, until the mushrooms begin to get glassy and soft, and are no longer releasing liquid. Add the turkey and the warm sauce, stir to combine, and cook until hot, approximately 7 to 10 minutes.

4. Stir in the sherry, then adjust seasonings. Serve over toast or white rice, garnished with finely chopped parsley.

TURKEY SALAD

Salad may have no place at the Thanksgiving table, but it can make for an extremely pleasant weekend-after-Thanksgiving lunch or light dinner. No real recipe is required—only a sense of proportion. Simply shred leftover turkey meat into a bowl with a healthy dollop of mayonnaise (the ratio is roughly a tablespoon to each cup of turkey meat), some diced celery (one stalk per cup!), minced scallion (a tablespoon per cup), and a healthy punch of fiery smoked paprika or the Californian chili-garlic sauce known as Sriracha (to taste). Serve in cups of Bibb lettuce, garnished with cilantro, with glasses of dry white wine. Spring is coming!

> *2 tablespoons mayonnaise*
> *2 tablespoons minced scallions*
> *2 stalks celery, cleaned and diced*
> *1 teaspoon smoked paprika or Sriracha, or to taste*
> *2 cups shredded leftover turkey meat*
> *Kosher salt and freshly ground black pepper*
> *4 whole leaves of Bibb lettuce*
> *2 tablespoons cilantro leaves*

1. In a medium-sized bowl, stir together the mayonnaise, scallions, celery, and paprika or Sriracha, then add the turkey meat. Stir lightly to combine. Add salt and pepper to taste, and add more paprika or Sriracha as desired.

2. Spoon a half-cup of salad into each Bibb lettuce leaf and garnish with cilantro.

—————— THANKSGIVING EGGS ——————

Exhaustive research into the business and culture of American breakfast suggests that you can always put an egg on it. Cold pizza? Heat in the oven while frying an egg to soft, yielding perfection. Slide it onto the slice and top with freshly ground black pepper: brunch. Is there some beef or pork or lamb sitting in the fridge after a dinner party? Sizzle up chunks of it with butter and diced potatoes and bell peppers, then serve with eggs on the side: brunch. Thanksgiving detritus is no different. Left-over dressing can be pressed into a pan and baked in the oven with eggs and a dusting of cheese to create a breakfast dish of remarkable heartiness and good flavor.

2 tablespoons unsalted butter
3 to 4 cups leftover Thanksgiving dressing
6 large eggs
2 tablespoons grated Cheddar cheese

1. Preheat oven to 400 degrees. Use the butter to heavily grease an 8-inch square baking pan and put into it the leftover dressing. Use the back of a spoon to press into this field of dressing 6 indentations into which you will later crack the eggs. Place the pan into the oven to heat for 10 to 15 minutes.

2. Remove heated dressing from oven and crack the eggs into the indentations. Sprinkle with the grated cheese and return to oven to bake until the eggs are just set, approximately 8 to 10 minutes. Serve with hot sauce and coffee.

TURKEY GUMBO

For some, this dish may be it, the whole reason to cook Thanksgiving in the first place. Turkey gumbo is a preparation common to south Louisiana, where the Cajun raconteur Pableaux Johnson has famously championed it: the very essence of turkey cooked down into hearty stock and thickened with roux, then topped full with andouille sausage and served over steamed white rice, with plenty of hot sauce on the side. Johnson drives the streets of New Orleans in the days following Thanksgiving to collect turkey bones from friends in order to make his stock, then invites the neighborhood over to dine on the gumbo he builds above it.

You need not go to such lengths. But do not stint on the time spent creating the roux, which should, when you are done with it, be almost the color of chocolate. Roux is the point of gumbo as plainly as turkey is the point of Thanksgiving. And remember that all gumbos improve in flavor after having been left to cure overnight in the refrigerator after cooking. Reheat over medium-low heat until the gumbo is hot, and serve with white rice. Garnish, as ever, with finely chopped parsley. Make this gumbo late on the weekend following the holiday—and feast for the coming week.

1 cup rendered turkey, duck, or chicken fat, if you
  have it, or a neutral oil like peanut or canola
1 cup all-purpose flour
2 large yellow onions, peeled and chopped
2 tablespoons "Creole" spices, or a mix of paprika, salt,
  celery salt, black pepper, cayenne pepper, onion
  powder, and garlic powder
2 stalks celery, diced
2 green bell peppers, cored, seeded, and diced
1 ripe tomato, seeded and chopped
4 cloves garlic, peeled and minced
2 pounds smoked pork sausage, andouille sausage, or
  kielbasa, sliced into thick coins
3 quarts final turkey stock (page 20) or chicken stock
2 bay leaves
2 tablespoons fresh thyme leaves

*2 or more cups shredded and chopped leftover turkey
    meat*
2 cups sliced fresh okra (optional)
1 to 2 tablespoons Worcestershire sauce, or to taste
Kosher salt and freshly ground black pepper

1. Make the roux. Pour the fat or oil into a heavy-bottomed pot set over high heat and let it get hot. Whisk the flour into the hot fat, then reduce heat to medium. (Be careful: it will sizzle and pop.) Continue to whisk until the roux takes on the color of coffee ice cream, approximately 20 minutes.

2. Add the onions, stirring them into the roux, and continue to cook, stirring often, until they are soft and the roux is the color of glossy chocolate, an additional 10 or so minutes.

3. Sprinkle the spices over the roux and onions and stir to combine, then add the celery, bell peppers, tomato, and garlic. Stir to combine, and cook until the vegetables have started to soften, approximately 5 minutes. Add the sausage, then the turkey stock, bay and thyme leaves, and bring the mixture to a boil. Reduce heat to low and cook for approximately 90 minutes, stirring occasionally.

4. Add leftover turkey meat, the sliced okra if you are using it, Worcestershire sauce, and salt and pepper to taste, and continue to cook an additional 15 to 20 minutes, until turkey is hot and flavors have started to meld. Adjust seasonings. Cure overnight and reheat, or serve immediately over white rice, with hot sauce on the side.

INDEX

Squanto, 7
squash
   Pumpkin Pie, 106–7
   Roasted Butternut, with Butter
     and Sage, 58–59
   soup, 9
   Steamed Butternut, with Butter
     and Parsley, 59–60
standing mixers, 13
Steamed Butternut Squash with
    Butter and Parsley, 59–60
Stewart, Martha, 86
stock, 10–11, 38, 70
   Quick Turkey Stock, 19
   Serious Turkey Stock, 21
   from the turkey carcass, 20
stuffing, 49
   See also dressing
sugar, 18
sweet potatoes, 12, 17, 57–58

the table
   condiments, 81, 84
   food stations, 84
   seating plans, 87
   settings, 78–84
tablecloths, 80
table salt, 16
teriyaki butter, 23, 24–25
thanks-giving, 86
Thanksgiving Eggs, 122–23
thawing guidelines, 34–35
thermometers, 31, 43
Three-Pepper Sausage Cornbread
    Dressing, 50–51
thyme, 17

timing the turkey, 31
Toby's Eggnog, 89–90
tongs, 13
tools, 13
turkey, 22–46
   brining, 29–30, 42, 45
   Butterflied Roast Turkey,
     35–36
   carving, 37–40
   cooked temperature, 25, 31
   cooking time, 31
   Deep-Fried Turkey, 43–44
   drippings, 11–12, 69
   Even More Simple Roast
     Turkey, 26–27
   Fast Roast Turkey, 35–37
   free-range turkey, 33
   fresh turkey, 32–33
   fried turkey, 41–43
   frozen turkey, 32
   Grilled Turkey, 29, 44–45
   Herb-Roasted Turkey, 27–29
   heritage turkey, 34
   kosher turkey, 33
   leftovers, 119–25
   organic turkey, 34
   pre-butchered roasting, 36–37
   roasting pans, 11–12
   rosemary-infused teriyaki
     butter, 23
   Simple Roast Turkey, 24–26
   Smoke-Roasted Turkey, 45–46
   stock, 19–21, 70
   thawing guidelines, 34–35
Turkey à la King, 120–21
Turkey Gumbo, 123–25

About the Author

SAM SIFTON is the national editor of *The New York Times*, that newspaper's former restaurant critic, and a food columnist for the Sunday *Times Magazine*. Before coming to the *Times*, where he has also worked as the culture editor and the editor of the Dining section, he worked as a newspaper reporter and editor, a teacher in the New York City public schools, a first mate on a century-old schooner, and a prep cook. Sam Sifton lives in Brooklyn with his wife and two daughters.

About the Type

This book was set in Garamond, a typeface originally designed by the Parisian typecutter Claude Garamond (1480–1561). This version of Garamond was modeled on a 1592 specimen sheet from the Egenolff-Berner foundry, which was produced from types assumed to have been brought to Frankfurt by the punchcutter Jacques Sabon.

Claude Garamond's distinguished romans and italics first appeared in *Opera Ciceronis* in 1543–44. The Garamond types are clear, open, and elegant.

NOTES

NOTES

NOTES

NOTES

NOTES

NOTES

NOTES